EASY UPGRADES>
BUILT-INS, SHELVES, AND STORAGE

FROM THE EDITORS OF **This Old House**

CONTENTS

PERFECT STORAGE SOLUTIONS

{ **LIFE COMES WITH** a lot of stuff—and that means you need a lot of places to put it. Built-ins can create order out of chaos: that jumble of wet coats, shoes, and backpacks by the door; the countertop clutter in the kitchen; papers piled high on your desk; toys scattered about the family-room floor; the mountain of clothes on your bedside chair. Cabinets, cubbies, and shelves provide places for all your necessities and, when used thoughtfully, allow you to find what you need every day. They're key to living well in your house.

Built-in storage pieces not only tuck into the architecture of your rooms, tapping unused corners, but also shape it—by building out the four walls, creating sight lines, directing traffic patterns, and even partitioning an open plan. Built-in furniture makes small rooms live larger by hugging a space's contours and freeing up as much floor area as possible. Open shelves and niches allow you to personalize your rooms by putting specially chosen objects on display. Tailored to the style of your house, well-designed storage becomes part of its fabric, adding one-of-a-kind charm that boosts your home's value.

Whether you're thinking about adding built-ins as a weekend project or as part of a larger remodel, you'll find loads of eye-catching inspiration and smart advice on the pages that follow, including Trim Tricks—easy ways to get custom looks that save you money. We've also included a dozen of our favorite how-to and step-by-step projects.

As America's top remodeling resource for more than 30 years, *This Old House* has added built-ins to dozens of houses with the cameras rolling and featured hundreds of smart storage ideas in *This Old House* magazine and at thisoldhouse.com. We're excited to share what we've learned with you in this book.

Note to readers Almost any do-it-yourself project involves risk of some sort. Your tools, materials, and skills will vary, as will conditions on your project site. This Old House and the editors of this book have made every effort to be complete and accurate in the instructions. We will, however, assume no responsibility or liability for injuries incurred in the course of the projects shown in this book. Always follow manufacturers' operating instructions in the use of tools and materials, check and follow your local building codes, and observe all customary safety precautions.

ORDERLY STORAGE
A wall of open lockers with cubbies above and below turns a back-entry hallway into a tidy mudroom. The solid-wood bench top runs under the window and through both sides of the built-in, tying the entire unit together.

CHAPTER 1>

ENTRYWAYS

What's the first thing everyone does immediately after walking into a house? Set something down. It might be a purse or a briefcase, an umbrella and a coat, or keys and sunglasses. Kids slip off their shoes and let their backpacks drop, all too often leaving both smack in the middle of the floor. The right built-ins can help organize all this stuff and more by creating a dedicated space for everything, truly streamlining your comings and goings. Read on for inspiring ways to put outerwear, bags, sports equipment, and other everyday gear in their place.

inside

1_ **Lockers and Cubbies**

2_ **Benches and Coat Racks**

3_ **Organizers, Pullouts, and Drawers**

FROM LEFT A deep base unit under a bank of lockers provides sitting room for shoe changes. Curved lower shelves make a backrest.

Ample 16-inch-deep cubbies are ideal for organizing a season's worth of athletic gear—and keeping a few dog treats handy.

A pocket door is a space-saving way to hide an alcove of mudroom built-ins from view.

A handsome half-wall of cabinets and shoe cubbies carves mudroom storage out of a main entry without compromising front-door formality or interior sight lines.

LOCKERS AND CUBBIES

BY FAR THE BEST SOLUTION to entryway clutter is a full-fledged mudroom. This helpful buffer zone allows for orderly exit and reentry, with plenty of storage for everyday essentials. But if a separate space isn't available, you can colonize a hallway, an alcove, or even one wall with open-front lockers for quick-deposit items. Try to include one for each family member, plus an extra or two for over-flow and guests. For maximum hanging capacity, use large curved hooks so that during messy weather—and parties—you can double or triple what each one can hold. Plan some shoe cubbies down below, ideally with waterproof trays to collect drips, mud, and dirt. And think about providing a surface for staging important items, like work papers or shopping lists, while you're readying to go outside. Well-designed mudroom-style built-ins will save you time every day.

NEAT CATCHALL
Metal bins, fabric-lined baskets, and color-coded boxes keep small items organized and eliminate cubby clutter. Beadboard offers a tougher surface than drywall in an area that takes a lot of knocks.

← Perforated-metal baskets hide contents while allowing air to circulate.

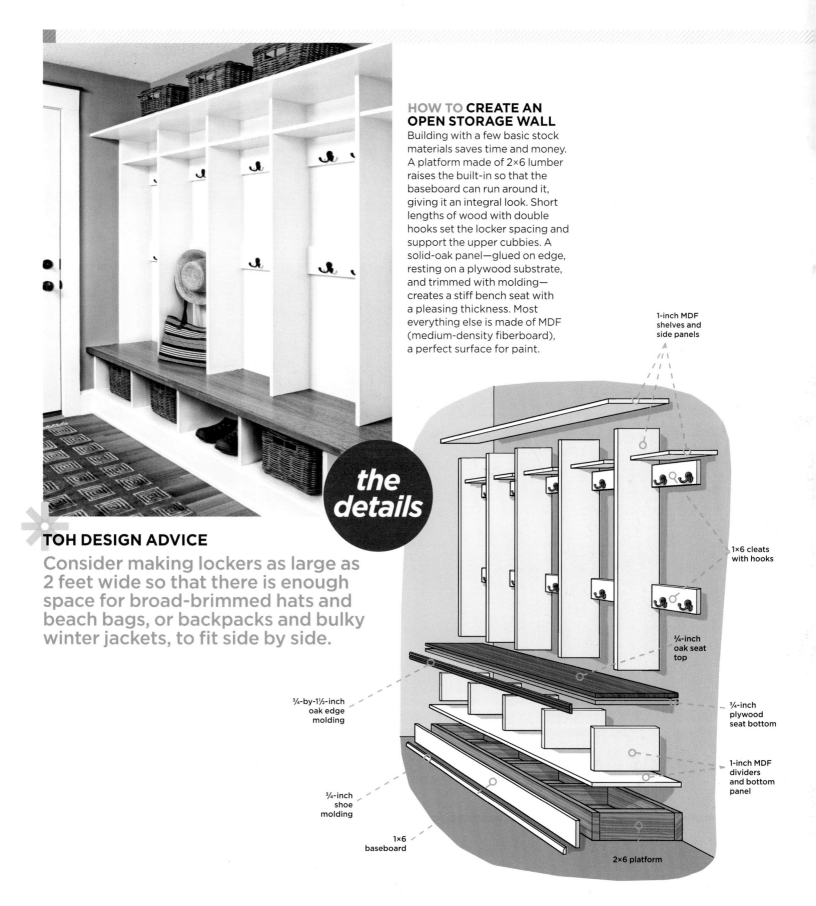

HOW TO **CREATE AN OPEN STORAGE WALL**

Building with a few basic stock materials saves time and money. A platform made of 2×6 lumber raises the built-in so that the baseboard can run around it, giving it an integral look. Short lengths of wood with double hooks set the locker spacing and support the upper cubbies. A solid-oak panel—glued on edge, resting on a plywood substrate, and trimmed with molding—creates a stiff bench seat with a pleasing thickness. Most everything else is made of MDF (medium-density fiberboard), a perfect surface for paint.

the details

TOH DESIGN ADVICE

Consider making lockers as large as 2 feet wide so that there is enough space for broad-brimmed hats and beach bags, or backpacks and bulky winter jackets, to fit side by side.

1-inch MDF shelves and side panels

1×6 cleats with hooks

¾-inch oak seat top

¾-inch plywood seat bottom

1-inch MDF dividers and bottom panel

¾-by-1½-inch oak edge molding

¾-inch shoe molding

1×6 baseboard

2×6 platform

→**CLEVER CURVES** Arched locker walls establish order while allowing for ample sitting room on the bench below. Matching seat supports create kick space to prevent anyone from tripping over them.

TRIM TRICK

Save money on stained-wood built-ins by using plywood rather than solid stock. Then hide exposed edges with self-adhesive veneer tape or solid-wood trim for a finished look.

↑**CUSTOM-HEIGHT HANGERS** Adjustable pegs allow family members to fine-tune their lockers as their storage needs change.

TRIM TRICK

Customize locker storage with a neat grid of pegboard holes on panels of painted MDF. Drill out the grids, and adhere to the backs of the lockers. Fit wood cabinet knobs with screws that are threaded on both ends. Finish with paint.

Upper cabinets are hinged at the top to make knobs more accessible.

Aligning a seat with a step is easiest when everything is built on-site.

FROM LEFT **Glossy oil-based paint is a good choice for an entryway built-in that gets sloshed with mud or snow.**

A row of hooks—here, fastened to a supersized window apron—eliminates having to add guests' gear to an already stuffed coat closet.

In a small alcove, creating a bench is simple: Just fasten it to the three surrounding walls like a sturdy shelf.

Curved "supports" under a bench seat echo the door's glass panel and the arched trimwork in this entry area.

BENCHES AND COAT RACKS

THE MESSIEST GEAR THAT COLLECTS AROUND ENTRYWAYS is outerwear, from muddy boots to snowy parkas. So if full mudroom built-ins aren't a possibility, go for two entryway essentials: a bench and a coat rack. The bench provides a spot to sit and exchange outdoor shoes for indoor slippers. Make it 16 to 18 inches high and deep to ensure easy and comfortable seating, and take advantage of the space inside or below the seat for storing footwear, either with a hinged lid, open cubbies, or a bank of shoe drawers. The coat rack can hang right above the bench or anywhere nearby, with hooks placed about 60 inches high. And if it's separate from the bench, you can add another row at 42 inches for kids. Just space the hooks 8 to 12 inches apart and stagger their placement so that the adults' jackets don't hang over the kids' hooks.

Entry-bench cushions will get wet, so cover them with outdoor fabric.

↑PERSONAL PULLOUTS In a back hall, bench drawers with labels for each family member hold shoes—after they've fully air-dried on the brick floor.

→SPACE-SAVER
Building in a bench alongside a central staircase makes a welcome resting spot in what would otherwise be wasted space.

TRIM TRICK
A return detail around the side of a plank seat gives it a traditional, well-crafted look.

→BARGAIN STORAGE
Notched metal strips, called shelf standards, paired with long shelf brackets offer an affordable way to create a DIY bench that grows with your family. Just add some pine planks for a seat with coat hooks above and rubber storage tubs below.

When adding a bench, stair returns may need to be trimmed to get a snug fit.

DIY project

If you're a capable do-it-yourselfer, you can build this bench in a weekend using the step-by-step instructions on the following pages.

BUILD A MUDROOM BENCH

Create a stopping area just inside the door so that people can change into and out of bad-weather gear and avoid tracking wet shoes into the house. Coming up: This Old House technical editor Mark Powers shows how

$ COST: $275

⊙ TIME: 18 HOURS

◆ DIFFICULTY: HARD

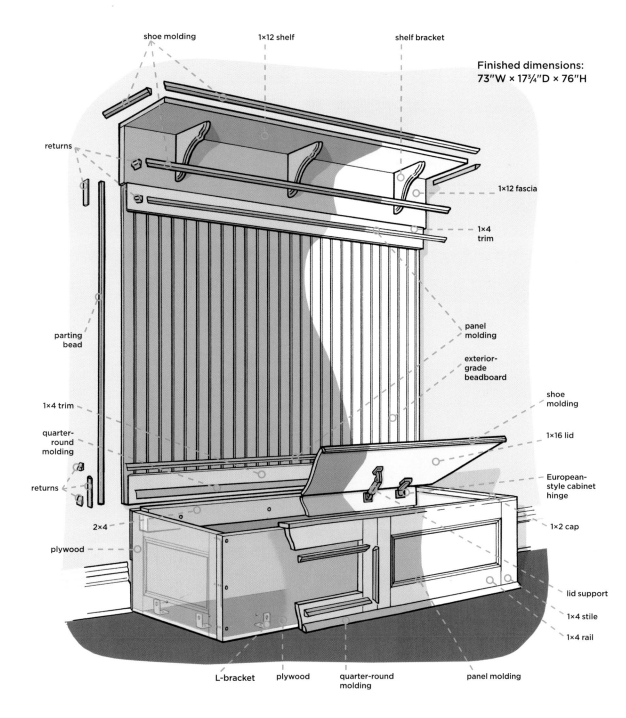

shoe molding

1×12 shelf

shelf bracket

Finished dimensions:
73"W × 17¾"D × 76"H

returns

1×12 fascia

1×4 trim

parting bead

panel molding

exterior-grade beadboard

1×4 trim

shoe molding

quarter-round molding

1×16 lid

returns

European-style cabinet hinge

2×4

1×2 cap

plywood

lid support

1×4 stile

1×4 rail

L-bracket

plywood

quarter-round molding

panel molding

TOOLS YOU'LL NEED >
- **circular saw**
- **drill/driver**
- **stud finder**
- **level**
- **miter saw**
- **hammer** and **nailset**
- **paintbrushes**

MATERIALS TO BUY >
- **¾-inch birch-veneer plywood** One 4-by-8-foot sheet
- **exterior-grade bead-board** One 4-by-8-foot sheet
- **1×16 solid-wood panel** One 6-footer
- **1×12 solid-wood panel** Two 6-footers
- **2×4** One 8-footer
- **1×4** Four 8-footers
- **1×2** One 10-footer
- **⅜-by-⅞-inch panel molding** Five 8-footers
- **½-by-¾-inch parting bead** One 8-footer
- **¾-inch quarter-round molding** One 16-footer
- **½-by-⅞-inch shoe molding** Three 8-footers
- **9-inch shelf brackets** Three
- **2-inch L-brackets** Seven
- **European-style cabinet hinges** Three
- **lid supports** Two
- **hooks**
- **1⅝-, 2½-, and 3½-inch deck screws**
- **2-inch trim-head screws**
- **2d and 3d finishing nails**
- **carpenter's glue**
- **vinyl adhesive caulk**
- **wood filler**
- **180-grit sandpaper**
- **primer** and **paint**

1_ INSTALL THE SEAT BOX.

Use a circular saw to rip two 16-inch-wide strips from the ¾-inch plywood, and cut them to length: two at 69½ inches and two at 15½ inches. Assemble the box with carpenter's glue and 1⅝-inch deck screws, overlapping the side panels with the front and back panels. Locate and mark the studs on the wall, and use a level to extend the lines 7 feet vertically. Cut away any base molding, position the box against the wall, and shim it level. Attach the box to the wall at the studs with 2½-inch deck screws and to the floor with L-brackets.

2_ INSTALL THE HINGE BLOCK.

Cut the 2×4 to fit the box's inside width (68 inches), then rip a 3½-inch-wide strip of plywood and cut it to the same length. Attach the plywood to the 2×4's face with 1⅝-inch deck screws. Set this assembly, plywood-side out, ¾ inch above the back of the box, and fasten to the studs using 3½-inch deck screws.

3_ ATTACH THE RAILS AND STILES.

Measure and cut eight 16-inch 1×4s for the stiles. Rip ¾ inch off one long edge of the two stiles that go on the front ends of the side panels, where they will be overlapped by the stiles on the ends of the front panel. Install all the stiles with glue and 3d finishing nails. Measure, cut, and install all the rails between the stiles. Measure and miter-cut lengths of panel molding at 45 degrees to fit inside the stiles and rails, and attach with glue and 2d nails.

4_ CAP AND TRIM THE BOX.

Cut the 1×2 to 71 inches and attach to the box's front lip with glue and 3d nails. Cut two pieces of 1×2 to 16¼ inches, and cap the sides, as shown. Trim the base with quarter-round molding, mitered at the front corners and cut square at the back, using glue and 2d nails.

5_ TRIM THE SEAT.

Use the 1×16 panel for the seat lid. Trim it with pieces of shoe molding, mitered at the front corners. Attach the molding to the lid's edges with glue and 2d nails.

6_ INSTALL THE LID.

Rip a 2¼-inch-wide strip of plywood, cut it to 72 inches long, and nail it to the back edge of the box to cap the hinge-block assembly from Step 2. Trim the ends of this cap with shoe molding. Attach the lid to the assembly using the three cabinet hinges (installing them according to the "full-overlay" instructions) and the two lid supports. The lid should overhang the box by about 1¼ inches on the sides and front.

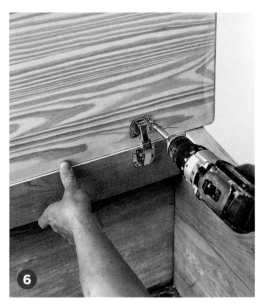

7_ MOUNT THE BEADBOARD.

Use a circular saw to cut the beadboard into two 4-by-4 panels. Mark a level line on the wall 4 feet above the seat. Position the panels between the line and the seat so that the joint falls over a stud. Mark where the panels meet the bench, and rip them to width. Attach them to the wall with adhesive caulk and to the studs with 2-inch trim-head screws.

8_ TRIM THE BEADBOARD.

Cut two 4-foot strips of parting bead, apply adhesive caulk, and use 3d nails to tack them in place against the side edges of the beadboard. Cut two 1×4s to mask the beadboard's top and bottom edges, but miter the ends (as you would for outside corners) so that the points extend past the parting bead. Attach with 3d nails, as shown.

9_ FINISH THE TRIM.

Finish the mitered 1×4 ends that overhang the beadboard with molding returns and adhesive caulk. To make a return, first cut a 45-degree miter for an outside corner into a 1×4 scrap. Set the miter-saw blade to 90 degrees, and cut the return to match the thickness of the beadboard and the 1×4 trim. Cover the joint where the two 1×4s meet the beadboard with mitered-and-returned panel molding. And where the 1×4 meets the lid, attach mitered-and-returned lengths of quarter-round molding to cover the joint.

10_ INSTALL THE FASCIA.

Mount a 1×12 panel above the beadboard by driving 2-inch trim-head screws into the studs, as shown.

11_ MOUNT THE SHELF BRACKETS.

Position the three shelf brackets—one centered and the others 4 to 6 inches in from each end—and mark the locations. Use the hardware provided to install them flush with the top edge of the fascia, centered over the marks. Trim the front and side edges of the 1×12 shelf with lengths of shoe molding—mitered at the front corners and cut square at the back—using glue and 2d nails. Secure the shelf to the brackets with 2-inch trim-head screws. Then cut a strip of shoe molding to length, mitered for outside corners, to go over the seam between the fascia and the 1×4. Flip it upside down, and nail over the seam. Install the returns with adhesive caulk.

12_ PAINT THE BENCH.

Apply wood filler to any holes, then sand, prime, and paint the bench. Mount the hooks using the provided hardware.

FROM LEFT By a kitchen door, a bank of oversize drawers with metal-mesh fronts holds shoes and backpacks.

This entryway organizer includes a shoe bench, slots for mail, and even an outlet for charging portable electronics.

A mail-and-key organizer is an easy entryway upgrade. This one is made from weathered wood planks and pegs.

Closed storage hides the mess inside. Chalkboard door panels offer a spot for reminders, and perforated-metal drawer fronts allow damp shoes to dry out.

ORGANIZERS, PULLOUTS, AND DRAWERS

IT'S THE LITTLE THINGS IN LIFE that matter most—especially the little things you can't find when you're trying to get out the door, like your car keys, sunglasses, or rain boots. So give these kinds of essentials a dedicated, easy-to-access home right by your most-used exit. A fairly simple closed cabinet or set of drawers organizes these and other important items—and tidies up the area of your home that visitors first see. Use interior dividers to keep things sorted and easy to find. Install an outlet, and your organizer can double as a charging station so cell phones, tablets, and portable GPS units are always fully juiced and ready to go. Behind doors or drawer fronts, even if the items inside do get jumbled up, the chaos will be hidden from view, helping to keep the peace in your household.

OPEN AND CLOSED
Tall cabinet doors conceal seasonal outerwear for the whole family. Rollout drawers with cutouts for grips shield contents from view while still offering a glimpse of what's inside. A few cubbies offer an opportunity for decorative display.

← **SLIDE-OUT RISERS**
In a compact back stairway, the space under the treads is put to good use as pull-out drawers for stowing kids' shoes and other small items. Knobs could be a tripping hazard, so these drawers open with flexible plastic tabs. Still to come: a railing to keep stair climbers steady.

→ **HIDDEN TRAY** The corner of a stair landing is anchored by a half-wall that holds light switches and display shelves. Its lid flips open to reveal an organizer for small items, including keys, wallets, sunglasses, and cell phones. It even has a charging station.

TRIM TRICK
Finishing a lid with decorative molding that has a rounded profile provides a convenient grip for opening it up.

→**MISSION ORGANIZER**
A built-in oak dresser gives everyday essentials a convenient hiding place in a formal entryway.

TRIM TRICK
To make new cabinetry look as if it has always been there, echo the material and finish of existing woodwork.

↑**KEY-AND-MESSAGE CENTER**
A simple pine-frame cabinet with a bulletin-board door panel creates a handy hideaway for keys, mail, the family calendar, and a shopping-list pad.

↑
Mirrored door panels offer a place for one last primp before heading out.

OUT-IN-THE-OPEN HIDEAWAY When storage space is needed near a main entry that is open to other rooms, hide everything behind doors and inside drawers and discreet containers.

CHAPTER 2 >
KITCHENS

Cabinets are the bones of a kitchen. They define the layout, determine traffic-flow patterns, and build in storage for all that cookware, cutlery, and china—as well as provide a base for your food-prep and snack stations. The average kitchen has 30 linear feet of these built-ins—including the upper and base runs, the island (if there is one), and any open shelving. Not only is cabinetry the biggest expense in building a kitchen, but this woodwork also gives the room its style and visual appeal. Read on to learn about your options.

inside

**1_ Cabinets and
Storage Islands**

2_ Open Shelving

FROM LEFT The door style defines a cabinet. Raised panels have a traditional look that can veer toward formal.

Sleek, modern slab doors downplay ornamentation but highlight your hardware choice.

Flat, or recessed, door panels have a classic look that can be plain and simple or, like these, dressed up with a bead detail.

Glass-panel doors with divided panes echo the windows in many vintage homes and put dishware on display.

CABINETS AND STORAGE ISLANDS

{ **THE MOST IMPORTANT THING** to understand about kitchen cabinets is that they're really just rows of modular boxes trimmed out to appear as unified built-ins. Manufacturers offer a range of styles, materials, and finishes in their stock lines, which doesn't necessarily mean they are literally in stock. With the exception of some home-center and flat-pack cabinets, they are generally made to order, in predetermined sizes, with trim strips to fill any gaps. Step up to a semi-custom line, and the maker will provide a greater selection of widths to fit your space. Custom cabinetry is designed from scratch to your particular plan, in nearly any wood, finish, style, and size that you can imagine—at about double the cost of stock and 50 percent more than semi-custom. Stick to stock and save, or spring for custom and get a unique look? Both offer a wealth of choices.

The end panels are inset, so they mirror the doors, minus the pulls. →

ACCENT ISLAND In a large kitchen with lots of storage, a bank of cabinets in a contrasting color breaks up what could otherwise be a monotonous look. This island draws the eye, thanks to its dark stained finish, colorful cookbook collection, and curved feet, copied from a vintage dresser.

Kitchen cabinet guidelines

Although they can be configured in myriad ways, cabinets are typically built and installed using well-established dimensions. Follow these rules of thumb in the planning stage to help you imagine how your cabinets will look and function.

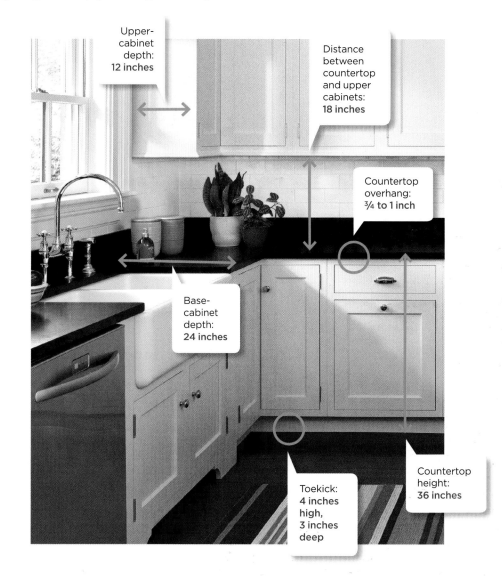

Upper-cabinet depth: 12 inches

Distance between countertop and upper cabinets: 18 inches

Countertop overhang: ¾ to 1 inch

Base-cabinet depth: 24 inches

Countertop height: 36 inches

Toekick: 4 inches high, 3 inches deep

TOH DESIGN ADVICE

To ensure that cabinets will last, order plywood construction, fully dovetailed drawers, and premium hinges and drawer glides.

↓**HIDDEN ASSETS** An island is not just for cabinet storage, it can also neatly house appliances, including ovens, dishwashers, or refrigerator drawers, often hiding them from view. This flip-up door conceals the microwave, conveniently located at a height that kids can reach.

Continuing the backsplash onto the sidewall protects the painted surface from spatters.

↑**UPDATED TAKE** The classic butler's pantry, a storage-lined passageway between a kitchen and a dining room, gets a fresh look here with hexagonal-wire-mesh panels on the upper doors and extra function with outlets for a cappuccino maker and other small appliances.

Painted green, the beadboard becomes the back wall of the glass-front cabinet. ↓

STUDY IN CONTRAST
A reclaimed-chestnut island and a salvaged-beadboard backsplash stand out against green-painted cabinets assembled into a hutch.

TRIM TRICK
If you want to make built-ins from salvaged wood, find a cabinetmaker who is experienced in working with its unique characteristics, from warped boards to visible nail holes.

The counter at the baking station is lower for greater comfort while rolling pastry.

← **TIME-HONORED**
A mix of glass and brass pulls, creamy yellow paint aged with a caramel glaze, an island made from salvaged wood, and a green plate-rack cupboard give the impression that this kitchen evolved over time.

TRIM TRICK
Order your crown moldings from the cabinet company to ensure a perfectly matched finish.

↑ **BUILT-IN ACCESS** To maximize storage space, the cabinetry reaches all the way to the ceiling. It is accessible with help from a rolling library ladder, which can be pushed up against the cabinets when not in use.

← **STORAGE EVERYWHERE**
Who says an island's knee space has to be wasted? Slide these stools away and you can access deep cabinets for special-occasion wares.

→ **REPURPOSED PIECE** In a converted carriage house, the island base was made from a workbench found in the building. It is topped with a limestone slab and cutting boards sliced from the bench's original scarred top.

↑ **WINE STORAGE** A built-in wine rack is a simple accessory that works in either a wall cabinet or a storage island.

Door-mounting options

Once you've chosen your doors, perhaps the biggest decision, both in terms of your cabinets' appearance and their construction, is how they will be mounted. Inset doors that sit inside prominent face frames—the strips of wood that cover the edges of the cabinet carcass—have the most traditional look. Today's standard choice is a partial-overlay door, in which the door slightly overlaps a narrow face frame. Or you can go for full-overlay doors with no face frames, if you want a more modern, streamlined style.

"Build in" the fridge with custom wood panels that match the cabinets.

1_ INSET Doors and drawers sit perfectly flush within the face frame. Hinges can be exposed or hidden. Here, the knuckles of the traditional butt hinges are visible alongside the door.

2_ PARTIAL OVERLAY The doors sit on top of the face frame, covering only a portion of it. This option allows for either hidden or exposed hinges.

3_ FULL OVERLAY The doors completely cover the front of the cabinet, so no face frame is required and hinges are hidden. This allows for the largest-size cabinet opening and makes cleaning inside easier.

FROM LEFT Chunky brackets, and paint that matches the wall trim, give these over-the-dishwasher dinnerware shelves the look of an original detail.

A low cookbook shelf with a stone top offers a sweet spot for display—and a place to set down a hot dish right next to the wood breakfast bar.

Got an odd spot to fill? A simple open-shelf unit can be made to fit, then painted and trimmed to match the rest of the kitchen cabinetry.

A plate rack is a charming way to keep dishware safe from chips—just place it within easy reach of the dishwasher to ease filling those slots.

OPEN SHELVING

THERE ARE LOTS OF ADVANTAGES to open shelves in the kitchen. They're more affordable than drawers or cabinets with doors because there's less material and labor involved. They put your gear—both utilitarian cooking tools and display-worthy serving pieces—out in plain sight. In that way, they save time and effort when you're preparing a meal. Rather than opening a cabinet door and rolling out a pull-out tray to grab a platter, you can simply pluck it off the shelf. But they're a magnet for clutter and dust if not used strategically. Beyond displaying a few cherished (or oversize) items, open storage works best for everyday coffee mugs, cereal bowls, and other dishware that you wash frequently, and for cookbooks, which are generally stored out in the open anyway.

→ **HARD WORKER** Lightened up with a pale palette, this kitchen is lined with cabinets and shelves, so no space goes to waste. The large island has both closed storage and open cookbook shelves framed by turned legs that also set off the snack counter.

↑ Open shelving cleanly frames above-the-sink windows and doesn't block natural light.

↑**CUSTOM WASHSTAND**
Turn the sink cabinet into an accent piece. This farm-sink base has turned legs and an open shelf for frequent-use pots and serving pieces. A zinc countertop and a faucet with Victorian-era styling complete its old-fashioned look.

Ebony knife blanks from a woodworking catalog were used to make the pulls.

↑AIRY LOOK To keep these dark-wood cabinets from feeling heavy, reeded-glass door panels and open shelving run across the tiled-to-the-ceiling storage wall.

←SLEEK LOOK
Not-quite-floating shelves straddle the line between modern and traditional when set against a wall of beveled subway tile.

TRIM TRICK Make these ebonized shelves by mortising stainless-steel brackets from a big-box store into stained maple planks. Be sure to fasten them into the wall studs.

→EASY ACCESS Cubbies and open shelves are a good choice for serious cooks because they put food-preparation and serving supplies within easy reach—much as you'd see in a restaurant kitchen.

↑
A substantial face frame outlines each cubby and inset drawer in this cabinet.

↑**OVER THE FRIDGE** Rather than the standard hard-to-access cabinet above the refrigerator, open shelves and cubbies that rise to the ceiling turn the space into valuable real estate for storage and display.

→**VINTAGE ECLECTIC**
These custom cabinets are modeled after furniture pieces to create an added-over-time, 19th-century look that also works beautifully for today.

→**END-CAP OPTION**
Farm-table-style legs at the four corners of this island frame a set of shelves that face the family room as well as a run of closed cabinets on the adjoining side.

Slide-out baskets keep potatoes and onions out of the sun and within reach.

COZY CORNER Paired with a petite bistro table, this curved banquette, or bench seat, turns the narrow end of a small kitchen into a compact spot for casual meals and cold refreshments.

CHAPTER 3>
DINING AREAS

There are dinner parties, with linen napkins and fancy platters. And then there are everyday meals, usually enjoyed somewhere other than the dining room table. Your house should comfortably make space for both, along with the host of non-food-related activities that happen in kitchens and informal eating areas—from doing homework to paying bills to playing board games. There are terrific built-ins to accommodate all these pursuits and meet any storage demands that go along with them. Just check out the creative ideas on the following pages.

inside

1_ **Banquettes and Booths**

2_ **Breakfast Bars**

3_ **Cupboards, Hutches, and Sideboards**

FROM LEFT Painted white and topped with wood, this dining area's flat-panel bench design coordinates with the kitchen cabinets.

A table supported by a simple pedestal makes getting in and out of a booth easy. Drawers in the ends of the benches offer access even during dinner.

Durable upholstery fabric treated to resist stains protects an active banquette area from the inevitable spills.

Colorful awning material ties this bench seat's cushions into the painted floor pattern and whimsical scalloped table.

BANQUETTES AND BOOTHS

EVER NOTICE THAT BOOTHS ARE THE FIRST TABLES to fill up at casual family restaurants? That's because they're the most fun, private spots in the place—like a clubhouse that encircles your family. A booth in or near the heart of your home—the kitchen—will also quickly become the household's preferred spot to eat everyday meals or just hang out. Best of all, booths work well in compact rooms because you don't have to provide floor space all the way around them for people to push back chairs or pass by. A full, two-sided booth in an alcove might take up just one-third as much space as a similar-size table and chairs. Build a single straight or L-shaped banquette, push a freestanding table in front of it with a chair or two on the other sides, and you may need only three-quarters of the square footage that a standard freestanding dining set requires.

A heat grille in the toekick ensures that diners stay toasty during cold weather. →

FOOT SAVER A bench seat that overhangs its base by a few inches allows people to tuck in their legs, push the table out, and let others pass without toes getting stepped on.

Banquette guidelines

Benches can be straight, L-shaped, even curved. Regardless of how they're configured, use the clearances below for maximum comfort and utility. When it comes to interior storage, a drawer in the end of the bench provides easiest access.

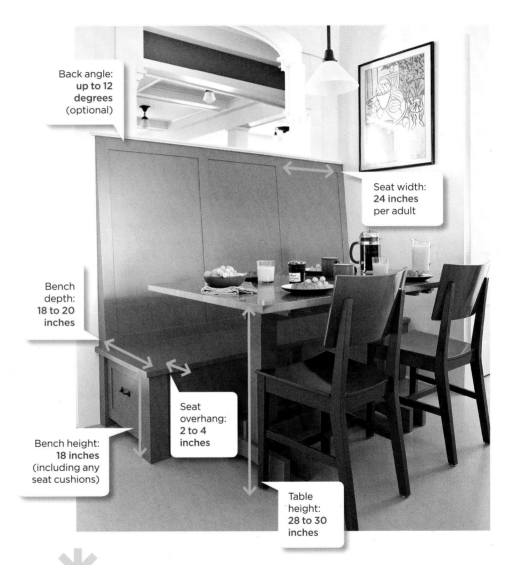

Back angle: **up to 12 degrees** (optional)

Seat width: **24 inches per adult**

Bench depth: **18 to 20 inches**

Seat overhang: **2 to 4 inches**

Bench height: **18 inches** (including any seat cushions)

Table height: **28 to 30 inches**

✳ TOH DESIGN ADVICE

For a booth that's roomy enough for the whole family to eat together, choose a pedestal or trestle table to ease getting in and out, and allot a 2-foot-square eating surface for each seat.

COUNTRY CHARM

Beadboard adds a cottage touch in a simple panel design. Highlight it further with a two-tone paint scheme.

TRIM TRICK

A rail at the end of the bench keeps cushions in place and gives a banquette a finished look. Rounding the edges creates a nice handhold for getting in and out.

← Framing an alcove with rustic timbers reinforces the special quality of the space.

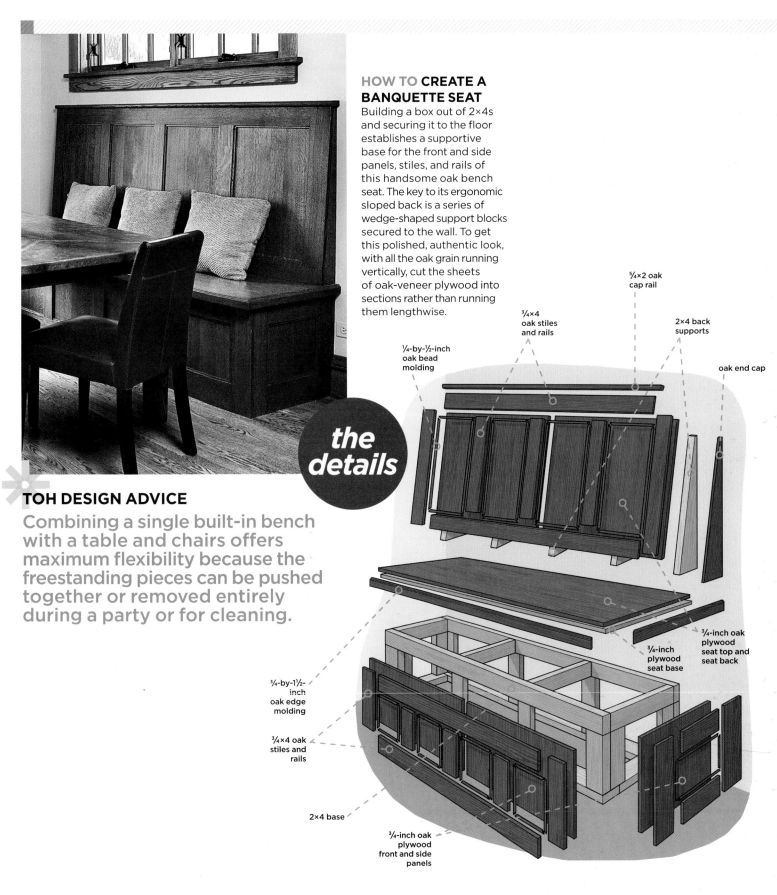

HOW TO **CREATE A BANQUETTE SEAT**

Building a box out of 2×4s and securing it to the floor establishes a supportive base for the front and side panels, stiles, and rails of this handsome oak bench seat. The key to its ergonomic sloped back is a series of wedge-shaped support blocks secured to the wall. To get this polished, authentic look, with all the oak grain running vertically, cut the sheets of oak-veneer plywood into sections rather than running them lengthwise.

TOH DESIGN ADVICE

Combining a single built-in bench with a table and chairs offers maximum flexibility because the freestanding pieces can be pushed together or removed entirely during a party or for cleaning.

the details

⁵⁄₄×2 oak cap rail

¾×4 oak stiles and rails

2×4 back supports

oak end cap

¼-by-½-inch oak bead molding

¾-inch oak plywood seat top and seat back

¾-inch plywood seat base

¾-by-1½-inch oak edge molding

¾×4 oak stiles and rails

2×4 base

¾-inch oak plywood front and side panels

→BOOTH WITH A VIEW A U-shaped bench in a bay-window alcove delivers maximum seating in minimal square footage as there is no need to provide space for chairs to push back from the table.

A wide, flat pedestal base may not need anchoring, so the table can pull out easily. ↓

↑MODERN JUKE JOINT A TV screen built into a booth isn't just for watching the morning news over coffee, it can also serve as a digital version of a diner classic: a controller for a whole-house music system that plays through speakers in the walls.

Banquette storage

If kitchen and dining room space are at a serious premium in your house, there's another advantage to a built-in bench: The space under the seat can provide a significant cargo hold for all sorts of gear. Access isn't easy—you'll likely have to remove the cushions or slide the table and chairs away to get at the compartments—so these hideaways work best for occasional-use items. These might include extra linens, giant platters, the juicer and pasta maker that you rarely fire up, or back-up bulk provisions from the warehouse store. Putting these things in an out-of-the-way spot will open up space in your main cabinets and closets for everyday needs.

1_ LIFT-UP DOORS
Rather than hinging the whole lid, create several smaller access panels to keep contents better organized and make them easier to retrieve.

2_ FRONT ROLLOUTS
Deep, wide drawers on full-extension glides can stow giant loads—but you'll have to move away the table when you want to get into them.

3_ BENCH RECESS
A simple alcove built into the end of a bench makes a perfect floor-level spot for a pet-bowl station.

FROM LEFT Adding an overhanging counter and a couple of inexpensive stools to a peninsula turns any kitchen into an eat-in kitchen.

Kids love the elevated vantage point of the family chef's work that they get when sitting on a counter-height perch.

A butcher-block counter allows a breakfast bar to double as a handy food-prep surface before cooking commences.

A wood bar top warms up a kitchen with long runs of stone counters. A protective clear coat makes it easier to wipe up spills and crumbs.

BREAKFAST BARS

A TABLE AND CHAIRS in the kitchen give you a place to eat, but they don't put you where the action is. That's why, when it's time to remodel, at the top of nearly every wish list is a generous work island or peninsula that has an overhang for some pull-up stools. Known as breakfast bars—though put into service all day long—these space-efficient eating areas work for informal meals, of course. But they also provide meal-prep and serving space, since stools can tuck out of the way when not in use and because they're at the same 36-inch height as the kitchen countertops or even, on occasion, 42 inches high, like the bar at the corner tavern. Breakfast bars invariably become gathering spots, too, not just for casual nibbles but also for quality time with kids and party guests, who can watch the chef at work or—even better—pitch in to help.

←ELEVATED APPROACH A two-tier island separates the working countertop from a dedicated breakfast bar that's six inches higher, keeping meal-prep and serving surfaces segregated. A raised bar also hides cooking clutter from view.

←TIDY TABLE Even in a narrow galley kitchen, the countertop may be able to turn at a tight right angle. Supported by a wall-hung bracket and a single turned leg, the open setup allows stools to slide in from multiple directions.

→WELL-STOCKED NOOK Serving ware and pantry supplies are within arm's reach for diners seated at a bar surface that extends out from a custom kitchen hutch.

↑HARD WORKER Maple butcher block offers a softer, warmer surface than stone, so it won't shatter dropped dishware or chill elbows or food on a wintry day. It's also forgiving of nicks and cuts, which can be sanded out.

→FARMHOUSE STYLE
For some traditionalists, today's big work island can look decidedly contemporary, but using a rustic wood top, painted base cabinets, and old-fashioned bin pulls can give it the look of classic kitchen furniture.

Recessed lights overhead are an unobtrusive way to brighten a wide breakfast bar.
↓

→PASS-THROUGH This kitchen and family room retain some separation thanks to wide arched openings and a curved breakfast bar that straddles both rooms.

TRIM TRICK
Off-the-shelf wood brackets are an inexpensive way to add character to an overhang, whether or not they're needed for support.

A top at a different height and turned table legs lighten up the look of a bar extension. →

→ **SINK SPACE** If you're putting a breakfast bar in front of an island sink (or cooktop), allow at least 24 inches of countertop clearance between the faucet and the edge that faces the stools.

A curved counter enables face-to-face conversation better than a straight run can. ↓

↑**AFFORDABLE SOLUTION** Finish a wide base cabinet with end panels and a butcher-block top that overhangs the sides for a budget-friendly setup. Just add a couple of stools from the home store.

Built-in tables

Most breakfast bars are built at counter height (36 inches), because they flow right into adjacent kitchen work surfaces. Others are raised to 42 inches, which allows you to reduce the overhang that's needed to accommodate a diner's knees from 15 inches to as little as 12 inches. Lower the bar to 30 inches, add a leg or two, and you've got a table-height extension, allowing adults to sit on a standard chair, feet on the floor, rather than perch on a bar stool. More dining station than workstation, these tables can accommodate seated food prep—just remember to factor in 18 inches of under-the-table space for people's knees.

1_ ISLAND EXTENSION
Attaching a table to a taller island keeps the combined footprint relatively compact and creates a handy neighboring serving area.

2_ WALL EXTENSION
Where eating-area space is tight, attaching the table to a wall on one side, peninsula-style, keeps passageways clear.

3_ DUAL HEIGHT
A built-in bar that runs along a step up to the kitchen allows extra dining chairs to be added on the table-height side as needed.

FROM LEFT Reinstalled as a built-in, this painted 1850 corner cabinet inspired the home's entire remodel.

Textural, pierced-tin cabinet-door inserts, reminiscent of a pie safe, can be swapped in for existing door panels.

Repainted and repurposed as a sideboard, an old pharmacy cabinet is ideal for storing flat supplies, like small trays, flatware, and linens.

Gold metallic paint draws attention to the stunning, concave interior of this 18th-century built-in.

CUPBOARDS, HUTCHES, AND SIDEBOARDS

SOME DINING-AREA BUILT-INS have a long precedent in the architecture of American homes. Corner cupboards, china hutches, and sideboard servers are cherished features of many period houses, especially those from the early 20th century, and adding them to a home of any vintage can imbue rooms with similar traditional charm. You can, of course, have a contractor build such cabinets from scratch, just as they did in the old days. But there are lower-cost and even do-it-yourself ways to get the same look at much less expense. Purchase a corner cupboard from an unfinished-furniture store, and finish it using standard lumber-yard trim. Make a custom sideboard by assembling a few stock kitchen cabinets and adding furniture feet. Or hit the flea markets for a freestanding antique cabinet, then build it in to create a one-of-a-kind dining-area display and storage piece.

→ **WET WALL** A wide floor-to-ceiling hutch extends kitchen storage to the eating area. It houses a small built-in coffee station with a sink and a tile backsplash for quick cleanup.

Two rows of wood dowels keep plates separated— and safer than if stacked. →

↑**HALLWAY HUTCH** An open-on-top cabinet between the kitchen and the breakfast area offers grab-and-go dishware storage in a plate rack, a polished wood countertop for setting down serving dishes, drawers for organizing cutlery, and shelves for piling up cookbooks.

→ **ACCENT PIECE**
A vibrant yellow painted-and-glazed finish calls extra attention to a custom hutch set against a neutral grass-cloth-covered wall.

TRIM TRICK
Keep a built-in's crown molding a few inches below the ceiling to enhance its stand-alone, furniture-like feel.

Ten coats of varnish protect the black-walnut counter from sink splashes.

69

AGED APPEARANCE
Pine planks, salvaged as-is from a centuries-old barn, give this new built-in corner cupboard a long-lived, antique look.

↓ HEATER HIDER

A radiator cover doubles as a sideboard with drawers for silverware and a marble top that helps keep pie at the perfect serving temperature.

TRIM TRICK

To enable a cabinet to sit flush against existing wainscoting, trace the piece's outline onto the baseboard and chair rail, then carefully cut them away using an oscillating tool with a saw blade.

↑ Perforated-metal panels allow the radiator's heat to flow into the room.

↑ **START WITH READY-MADE** To get a custom look at a bargain price, buy a unit from an unfinished-furniture store, and build it in with stock trim along the sides and additional decorative molding along the top. Then paint the assembly to match the rest of the trim in the room.

TRIM TRICK

To make a corner cabinet look like an integral part of a room's architecture, remove wainscoting or chair rails on adjacent walls, or wait to install them until after the piece is in place, so that the woodwork can overlap the cabinet's sides.

BUILD A SIDEBOARD FROM KITCHEN CABINETS

You can enhance stock cabinets with molding, furniture feet, and knobs to build a sideboard for a fraction of the cost of buying one ready-made. This Old House general contractor Tom Silva shows you how

DIY project

It takes about a day's work to build this affordable sideboard using unfinished base cabinets that have doors and operable drawers.

$ COST: $400

TIME: 8 HOURS

DIFFICULTY: MODERATE

TOOLS YOU'LL NEED>
- **combination square**
- **straightedge**
- **handsaw**
- **drill/driver**
- **circular saw**
- **hammer** and **nailset**
- **screwdriver**
- **miter saw**
- **putty knife**
- **paintbrush** and **roller** with ⅜-inch-nap cover

MATERIALS TO BUY>
- **18-inch base cabinets with doors and drawers** Three
- **1×3 furring strips** Two 10-footers
- **½-inch Baltic birch plywood** Two 4-by-8-foot sheets
- **½×1 lattice strips** Two 6-footers
- **½×2 lattice strips** Two 8-footers
- **¾-by-1⅛-inch base cap molding** One 8-footer
- **corner foot plates** Four
- **furniture feet** Four
- **drawer knobs** Six
- **magnetic push latches** Three
- **1⅝-inch deck screws**
- **2d and 3d finishing nails**
- **carpenter's glue**
- **construction adhesive**
- **wood putty**
- **medium-grit sandpaper**
- **primer** and **paint**
- **gold metallic wax**

Finished dimensions: 59½"W × 25⅛"D × 35½"H

plywood top

base cap molding

furring strips

18-inch base cabinet

½×2 lattice strip

½×1 lattice strips

corner foot plate

furniture foot

1_ REMOVE THE TOEKICKS. Using a combination square and a straightedge, transfer a line that is flush with the bottom edge of the face frame to the toekick, sides, and back of each cabinet. Cut along this line with a handsaw and remove this excess material.

2_ FASTEN CABINETS TOGETHER. Sandwich two furring strips, cut to length, vertically between the cabinets to act as spacers. Using a drill/driver and 1⅝-inch deck screws, fasten the cabinets together along the length of the strips. For added strength, sink the screws from both sides.

3_ COVER THE ENDS. Use 3d nails and construction adhesive to fasten two furring strips vertically to each end of the joined cabinets, front and back. If the face frame extends beyond the unfinished end, set the front strip behind it, as shown. Using a circular saw, cut two pieces of plywood to cover both ends. Secure them to the strips with more adhesive and finishing nails.

4_ TRIM THE FRONT. Cut a ½×1 lattice strip 1 inch longer than the width of the joined cabinets. Center it horizontally on edge between the drawers and cabinets, and attach with wood glue and 3d nails. Hide the cabinet spacers and exposed plywood edges with vertical ½×2 strips fastened with glue and 2d nails. Glue and nail three ½×1s on the flat to the cabinet's bottom rail between the vertical pieces.

5_ ATTACH FEET AND HARDWARE. Screw on the corner foot plates, twist on the feet, and flip the piece upright. Drill holes for each pair of knobs, centering them vertically, about 4 inches in from each end, and screw the knobs in place. For each latch, glue and nail a block against the back of the face frame where the push latch will go, and mount it flush with the frame's front. Screw the latch in place with its plate attached. Mark the back of the plate with chalk, and close the door. Screw the plate to the back of the door at the chalk mark.

6_ MAKE AND TRIM THE TOP. Using a circular saw, cut plywood to match the top's width and depth, including all trim. Secure with adhesive and 2d nails, then recess the heads with a nailset. Trim the top with base cap molding, mitered at the front corners and cut square at the back, using glue and 2d nails. Fill seams and holes with wood putty. Sand smooth with medium-grit sandpaper, then prime and paint the sideboard. Highlight details with metallic wax, such as Rub 'N Buff.

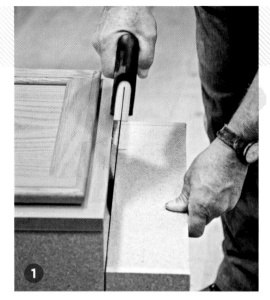

FIRESIDE STORAGE
Two bookcases flanking the hearth are joined by a single full-length top, turning a featureless painted-brick fireplace surround into an architectural focal point.

CHAPTER 4 >
LIVING AREAS

Gone are the days, if they ever really existed, of formal living rooms, where everyone sat straight and children spoke only when spoken to. Today, we use these areas—living rooms, family rooms, and TV rooms—all the time and for all sorts of activities. And that's where built-ins can help, by displaying or hiding the diverse gear we need, from media equipment to board games and books to bar supplies. The following pages hold a whole range of ideas for enhancing these areas in your own home.

inside

1_ **Bookshelves, Display Cases, and Storage**

2_ **Media Cabinets**

3_ **Built-in Bars**

FROM LEFT **Though period wall niches typically have concave interiors, an easier-to-build flat back actually works better for displaying books and artwork.**

Substantial stepped-back built-ins in a family room take on a casual feel with some wire-mesh door panels that show off favorite knickknacks.

Outdated Colonial scrolled tops were covered with a plain valance board and crown molding to give this built-in a clean new look.

A chimney bumpout often results in a pair of living room alcoves that are tailor-made for a set of matching built-ins.

BOOKSHELVES, DISPLAY CASES, AND STORAGE

THE VERY PERMANENCE OF A BUILT-IN BOOKCASE or curio cabinet adds tremendous character to your home. Enormously flexible, custom shelves and cubbies can fit just about anywhere and hold just about anything. In addition to familiar locations, such as lining a wall or flanking a fireplace, a bookcase can create an alcove, surround a window, or gracefully divide a room in two. You don't need to pay a carpenter or a woodshop big bucks to add built-in shelving to your home, however. If you're handy, you can do the job yourself with just a few common tools, like a circular saw and a drill, plus the right construction material for what you're storing. Hardcover books are heavy, as are many objets d'art. You want to ensure that you'll have stable shelving that won't sag under the weight.

→ STOCK PLAN This built-in actually comprises two banks of flat-pack cabinets from a big-box store with trim across the top—and a couple of coats of green paint—to tie them together.

↑ OVERMANTEL AND SHELVES Building out the wall on either side of the chimney with cabinets and a soffit yields open and closed storage. These bottom cabinets are lined with metal to hold firewood.

TRIM TRICK

A great way to make any cabinet look built-in, as if it has always been there, is to tie it directly into any adjacent window casings.

→ DISPLAY CORNER Wall-to-wall windows that meet in a corner leave room underneath for a simple L-shaped bookcase, with its top serving as the windowsill.

A thin MDF box creates a beefy shelf for large display items. ↓

The window casing was cut so that the cabinets fit snugly, making an alcove for the sofa. ←

To eke out every inch of depth, skip back panels and attach a frame directly to the wall.

BUILT OUT On a large expanse of wall, adding bookshelves creates a niche for a favorite piece of furniture, such as this antique desk.

HOW TO **CREATE A SMALL BOOKCASE**

Fluted casing along the sides, decorative chair rail around the top, and chunky trim wrapping the base turn this basic assembly of cut-to-size parts into a handsome piece of furniture. Key to making these shelves sturdy is cutting them from stable ¾-inch MDF and using the same for the shelf supports. If you plan to fill your bookshelf with heavy items, such as numerous hardcover books, add shelf supports along the back panel as well.

TOH DESIGN ADVICE

To determine whether shelves should be made from MDF, plywood, pine, or oak—taking into account their span and what you plan to store on them—search "sag calculator" online before you finalize your project's design.

the **details**

¾-inch MDF top

¼-inch plywood back panel

1×4 rail

½-by-¾-inch parting bead

¾-by-2⅜-inch chair-rail molding

½-by-2¼-inch fluted casing

¾-inch MDF shelf supports

¾-inch MDF shelf and side panel

1×4 baseboards

→**ECONOMY OF SCALE** If a cabinetmaker is already on-site for a major kitchen remodel, ask him to add living room built-ins at the same time. Saving him a trip should yield a better price.

TRIM TRICK
Painting cabinets means mixing different materials is no problem, since in the end they will be finished to match.

↑**COZY AND WELL LIT** Glass-front cabinets and shelves of different thicknesses accommodate books alongside the fireplace—and provide an opportunity to run wiring for sconces without having to open up walls.

Painted wood cabinet tops look seamless and are far less costly than stone.
↓

A mix of drawers and doors keeps a wall of built-ins from looking monolithic.
↑

FROM LEFT **Arrange a built-in's openings so that the center of the TV screen is at eye level when you're on the couch.**

Handsome Prairie-style slatted doors are a clever way to provide essential ventilation to prevent home-theater electronics from overheating.

An angled TV-cabinet built-in that wraps a corner facilitates good viewing from anywhere along a large sectional sofa.

A working kitchen hutch offers a subtle yet convenient spot for the family chef to catch the evening news.

MEDIA CABINETS

DOES YOUR TV ROOM look like a warehouse for audio-visual equipment? A built-in entertainment center can house your flat-screen TV, cable box, receiver, wireless movie-streaming device, and gaming console, all in one space-saving place—with nary a cable or cord to be seen. Close the doors and all the components disappear, leaving you with cabinetry that's attractive enough for the formal living room. On the inside, you can include a variety of specialized media-centric features. For example, rollout shelves provide easy access to the backs of electronic components, for those times when you need to change the wires or unplug something for a hard reboot. And adjustable cubby and drawer dividers will neatly store DVDs or video-game cartridges. Finally, consider built-in speakers for a surround-sound experience and bifold or flipper doors for unobstructed viewing.

→ MONEY-SAVER
Limit the complicated
cabinetry to what is
needed to support the
TV and its peripherals,
and hang simple site-built
shelves next to and over
the screen.

TRIM TRICK
Continuing the room's
baseboard around a built-
in makes it feel like an
original part of the house.

↑**CLOSE QUARTERS** Even a modest armoire cabinet
can host a midsize TV, which is all you need when the seating
is close to the screen. A 37-inch screen can suffice when
you're sitting just 5 to 8 feet away. Wraparound, 270-degree
hinges allow doors to open fully for unobstructed viewing.

→**SEAMLESS
SURROUND** A large
media built-in with a
center panel eases TV
installation because it
hides the wiring without
having to break into the
wall. Fabric door and
drawer panels conceal
speakers and remote-
controlled components.

Inset doors and exposed hinges give built-in cabinetry a traditional look. →

←PIVOTING PANELS Flipper doors, which open 90 degrees and then slide into the cabinet, allow the television to be either hidden away or viewable from every seat in the room.

TRIM TRICK Surrounding classic vertical beadboard with strips installed diagonally creates a dynamic contrast.

→NOW YOU SEE IT A motorized lift, built into a room-dividing cabinet and operated with a universal remote control, raises and lowers a flat-screen TV— an ingenious solution in an open-plan space. A matching wood strip on the top hides the TV when it is lowered into the wall pocket.

COLOR TIE-IN This living room's warm stained woodwork and black soapstone fireplace surround keep a large TV screen from becoming a noticeable black hole when it is turned off.

A continuous soapstone top ties the fireplace and cabinetry together. ↓

BUILD A WALL-HUNG TV CABINET

A large TV is a must for the big game, but a large blank space on your wall isn't quite so captivating the rest of the time. To conceal it, build a cabinet with TOH technical editor Mark Powers

$ COST: $150

⏱ TIME: 4 HOURS

⑦ DIFFICULTY: EASY

DIY project

TOOLS YOU'LL NEED>

- clamps
- circular saw
- rafter square
- drill/driver
- miter saw
- brad nailer
- screwdriver

MATERIALS TO BUY>

- **1-inch-thick wood bifold door** One. To determine its size, add 4 inches to the TV's width, divide by 2, then round up to the nearest stock width.
- **1×6** (or a board a bit wider than the thickness of the TV) One 8-footer
- **1×8** (or a board about 2 inches wider than the previous piece) One 10-footer
- **1×4** Two 6-footers
- **bifold-door hinge** One, plus the three that come with the door
- **H-hinges** (for flush-mounted doors) Four
- **magnetic catches** Two
- **⅝-inch no. 4 flathead wood screws**
- **1½-inch wood screws**
- **3-inch deck screws**
- **1½-inch 18-gauge nails**
- **carpenter's glue**

Television sizes are based on the diagonal width of the screen, not the actual width of the unit. So before you select bifold doors, take an accurate measure of your TV.

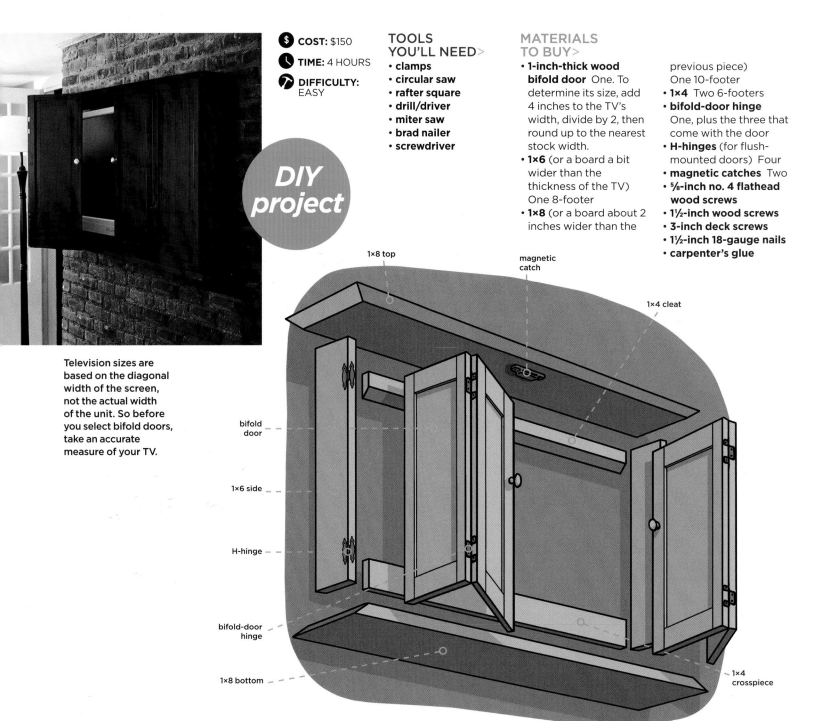

1×8 top

magnetic catch

1×4 cleat

bifold door

1×6 side

H-hinge

bifold-door hinge

1×8 bottom

1×4 crosspiece

1_ CUT THE DOORS. Remove the door hinges. Measure and mark a line through the center of each segment's middle rail, and cut along it with a circular saw. Use a rafter square to ensure a 90-degree cut.

2_ ATTACH THE BIFOLD HINGES. Hold two panels back-to-back, and line up each hinge so that its knuckle sits 4 inches from one end of the door. Mark the location of all screw holes, and drill pilot holes at each mark. Mount the hinges with ⅝-inch wood screws. Repeat for the second door.

3_ CUT THE CABINET PIECES. Lay the doors flat with a ⅛-inch gap between them. Measure their combined width and add 3½ inches. Cut both the 1×8s to that length using a miter saw. Set its blade at 45 degrees to create a bevel at each end. Cut the 1×6s without bevels, ¼ inch longer than the doors. Now use a circular saw to rip 45-degree bevels on the front edges of the 1×8s.

4_ ASSEMBLE THE CABINET. Position the 1×8s so that their bevels angle inward toward each other, and sandwich the 1×6s between them. Use the doors to determine the exact location of the 1×6s. Fasten the pieces together using 1½-inch wood screws driven into pilot holes. Set a circular saw to 45 degrees and rip a 1×4 down the center to create two cleats with mirrored bevels. Glue and nail one to the underside of the top board, flush with the back edge and with the beveled edge angling down toward the back of the cabinet. Glue and nail a 1×4 crosspiece to the back edge of the bottom board.

5_ ATTACH THE DOORS. Lay the frame on its back, and place wood blocks to hold the doors flat on top of the frame. Center the doors and position the H-hinges 4 inches from the top and the bottom. Drill pilot holes, and screw the hinges in place with ⅝-inch screws.

6_ ATTACH THE HARDWARE. Mark where the closed doors meet on the top and bottom boards. Position the magnetic catches, with their plates attached, 1 inch behind the marks to allow for the thickness of the doors. Screw the catches in place. Mark the backs of the plates with chalk, and close the doors. Screw the plates to the backs of the doors at the chalk marks. To hang the cabinet, screw the other cleat to the studs, with its beveled edge angled up and away from the wall, using 3-inch deck screws. Then hook the cabinet's cleat over the wall's cleat.

FROM LEFT A salvaged back bar mixes with a new concrete countertop in an 1890s farmhouse that once housed a pub.

A curved serving station, streamlined stools, and globe pendants give this living room bar an Art Deco flavor.

An in-kitchen beverage station stows barware and bottles of wine conveniently next to the camouflaged fridge.

Adding a small sink to a family-room cabinet gives you a place to store and serve—and clean up—for cocktail parties.

BUILT-IN BARS

{ **FORGET ABOUT REC-ROOM BARS** down in paneled basements, flanked by dartboards and beer-stein collections. Today's bars sit in high-visibility spots right off the kitchen, dining area, or living room, and they often feature custom cabinets and top-of-the-line fixtures and fittings. Some are plumbed butler's pantries that serve up mixed cocktails and hors d'oeuvres. Others are simply well-appointed cabinets, designed for storing wine and liquor and the glassware needed to serve them. And then there are modern takes on sit-down bars, a growing trend among homeowners who want a grown-up hangout zone for friends and family that's a little less workaday than the kitchen. Whichever type you choose, bar cabinets can store far more than shot glasses and single malts. Wine fridge, kegerator, ice maker, dishwasher, television—take your pick of pub-worthy accessories.

↑BUTLER'S BAR A walk-through pantry or a passageway adjoining the family room makes an ideal spot for a wet bar, complete with a refrigerator and a dishwasher. Rich woodwork makes it dressy enough to be on display for guests.

→SERVING STATION Water rings and wear only enhance the patina of an elevated bar counter made from rustic barn wood. Modern stools and the stained plywood panels that wrap the bar's base add a contemporary feel.

→SMART THINKING A pale marble counter, glass shelves, and mirrored walls make a bar in a converted closet feel luxurious and airy.

TRIM TRICK
With a mirrored wall, adding a backsplash made from extra countertop material eases cleanup.

An L-shaped bar allows for clear passage in front and seated serving on the side.

95

→ **TINY FOOTPRINT**
A one-bottle-deep shelving unit, hidden behind a sliding door in a sitting room, holds all the essentials for serving cocktails.

When closed, the sliding door's wire-mesh panel offers just a hint of what's inside. →

↑**PIPE ACCESS** Follow your plumbing lines across the basement, and you might discover that they pass right under a closet, a niche, or a cabinet—offering an easy way to upgrade the space to a wet bar.

Space-saving bar cabinets

If a full-scale wet bar just won't fit, you can squeeze the essentials into a single cabinet or two—either behind closed doors in a formal space or out in the open in a casual area. Since cork-stoppered wine bottles must be stored horizontally to avoid spoilage, standard upper cabinets won't work if you want to hide wine behind doors. Liquor bottles and stemware can stand vertically, however: Allow about 14 inches in height for bottle shelves and 11 to 12 inches for stemware. If there's no countertop, leaving a little hand-height cabinet space unused can provide a hidden work surface for mixing drinks. Mount a bottle opener and a wine corker inside to further simplify serving.

1_ PERFECT FIT Custom open cubbies, precisely built to accommodate glasses, wine bottles, and cocktail gear, create an orderly display.

2_ BASE-CABINET INSERT Clever behind-the-door dividers keep wine bottles lying down to preserve their corks, leaving plenty of room for liquor bottles on top.

3_ PULL-OUT STORAGE Rollouts with dividers turn a base cabinet into a spot for towels and bottles and barware that can stand up. There's even a cutting board for garnishes.

CHAPTER 5 >
ROOM DIVIDERS

Remodeling a house often means removing an interior wall or two to create a more open, family-friendly floor plan that better accommodates the way we live today. But where a wall once stood, something new is often needed to take on the structural load, to help segregate the now-adjoining rooms, or to do both. Using built-ins to reshape the architecture of open spaces gives them a custom, finished feel while adding useful storage shelves or cabinets. The ideas on the following pages may just inspire details for your own home.

inside

1_ **Columned Half-Walls**

2_ **See-Through and Floating Partitions**

FROM LEFT **Stand-alone base cabinets finished with columns separate the kitchen from the family room while allowing conversation to flow.**

When a column is just for show, it doesn't need to continue into the cabinet, leaving plenty of interior space for display items.

A subtle arch overhead, a tapered post, and a wainscoted half-wall distract from all the supports in this structurally complex corner.

Glass-door cabinets reduce the housekeeping load because dust does not collect inside them.

COLUMNED HALF-WALLS

WE TEND TO THINK OF COLUMNS as structural necessities, concessions to the force of gravity. So when a wall comes down, the hope is to avoid needing any visible posts in its place. But when paired with a low cabinet or a half-wall, columns become such striking interior-design elements that you might just want one or two even where there's no load to support. We owe this "colonnade" look to early-20th-century homes—especially bungalows, Colonial Revivals, and American Foursquares—and their architects, who made columns such popular features that they were sold as mail-order kits through builders' catalogs of the era. You can find recycled originals at salvage yards or build one new to fit between kitchen and family room, foyer and living room, or wherever you need just a little separation between contiguous spaces.

↑HALLWAY STORAGE Full-height coat cabinets transition to a half-wall of drawers and doors for accessories, allowing views into the adjoining room. Adding a mirror onto the side of the tall cabinet lightens up the look of the floor-to-ceiling portion of the storage unit, making it almost disappear.

→BUFFET WALL A bank of bar-height, 12-inch-deep cabinets—used for china and table linens—backs up to the kitchen's base cabinets in a post-and-beam home.

TRIM TRICK
Give the end of a cabinet run a polished look with additional cabinet doors, or glue down ½×2 lattice strips to mimic the style of divided-panel doors, as shown.

Stained doors and drawer fronts pick up the tone of the rustic timber frame.

A half-wall of cabinets wraps this beefy post so that it doesn't impede traffic flow.

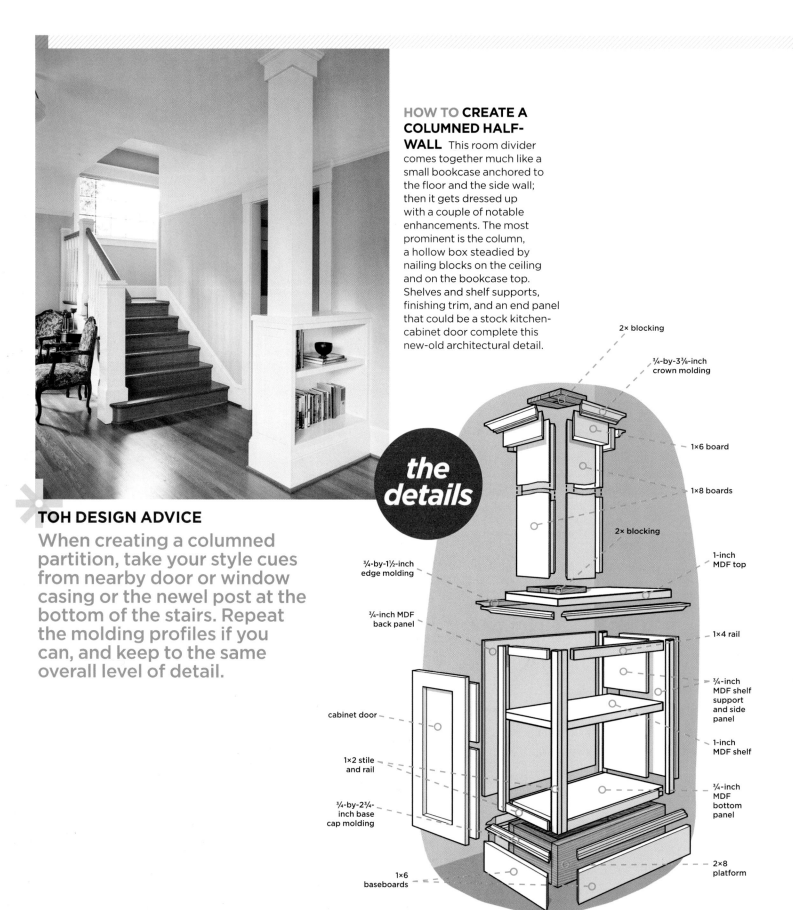

HOW TO **CREATE A COLUMNED HALF-WALL**

This room divider comes together much like a small bookcase anchored to the floor and the side wall; then it gets dressed up with a couple of notable enhancements. The most prominent is the column, a hollow box steadied by nailing blocks on the ceiling and on the bookcase top. Shelves and shelf supports, finishing trim, and an end panel that could be a stock kitchen-cabinet door complete this new-old architectural detail.

TOH DESIGN ADVICE

When creating a columned partition, take your style cues from nearby door or window casing or the newel post at the bottom of the stairs. Repeat the molding profiles if you can, and keep to the same overall level of detail.

the details

Labels (top to bottom, right side):
- 2× blocking
- ¾-by-3⅜-inch crown molding
- 1×6 board
- 1×8 boards
- 2× blocking
- 1-inch MDF top
- 1×4 rail
- ¾-inch MDF shelf support and side panel
- 1-inch MDF shelf
- ¾-inch MDF bottom panel
- 2×8 platform

Labels (left side):
- ¾-by-1½-inch edge molding
- ¾-inch MDF back panel
- cabinet door
- 1×2 stile and rail
- ¾-by-2¾-inch base cap molding
- 1×6 baseboards

FRAMING THE VIEW A low partition wall anchors a kitchen island on one side and backs a family-room bench on the other—while keeping sight lines open.

TRIM TRICK
Cladding a partition wall in hard-wearing beadboard protects it from scuffs and dents in a high-traffic area.

FROM LEFT A partial wall with built-in sconces and side tables allows the bed to float in the middle of a room that's lined with door and window openings.

Ceiling-hung cabinets with glass doors on both sides channel light between kitchen and family room. A built-in arch provides extra clearance over the sink.

Repeating the trim around the doorway, this built-in hutch allows glassware and serving dishes to show through.

The smaller the cubbies—and the bigger the items displayed inside—the greater the visual barrier that a grid of open shelving will create.

SEE-THROUGH AND FLOATING PARTITIONS

{ **MOST BUILT-INS—FROM WINDOW SEATS** to corner cupboards to kitchen booths—live in the natural nooks and alcoves of a house. By fitting into the building's contours, they turn forgotten and underutilized spaces into valuable assets. But custom cabinetry can also be built right in the middle of a wide-open area, where no store-bought piece of furniture could ever look right. A floating partition wall, for example, can define where one room ends and the next begins, but without obscuring the feeling of openness between, say, a master bedroom and an adjacent sitting area. Similarly, see-through cabinetry—open cubbies, shelves that have no backs, or cabinets with glass doors on both sides—can divide the kitchen from the dining room, for example, while allowing as much or as little integration as you want, depending on how substantial you make the woodwork.

Attractive and practical serving pieces are easily reachable from either room.

KITCHEN WALL
Two-sided upper and lower kitchen cabinets help to define the formal dining-room space without compromising the sight lines from the kitchen.

↑ PASS-THROUGH
Part wet bar, part display cabinet, and part sideboard, this walnut, maple, and mahogany built-in room divider lets food and drink move easily between kitchen and dining room.

→ OLD-SCHOOL UPDATE
In addition to helping separate the appliance-filled pantry from the kitchen, this cherry hutch frames an opening for back-to-back sinks and has two-sided dish and stemware storage up top.

Ornate styling and a stained finish distinguish the hutch from the kitchen cabinets. →

→ **TWO-WAY CUPBOARD**
With access from both the kitchen and the family room, a custom hutch offers a finished face to each room.

TRIM TRICK
Wrapping the sides of a drywalled passageway with wood casing protects corners from damage. Crown molding set at the same height as the room-dividing hutch gives the casing a natural end point.

The vanity base slants inward for a stylish way to create more foot room. →

↑ **BATHROOM ISLAND** With the tub on one side and the sink on the other, a freestanding built-in wrapped in walnut beadboard has a somewhat porous dividing wall—a mirror floating between two partition panels—that separates the grooming and relaxation zones.

The cabinet is accessible through doors and drawers on both sides.

AGED TO PERFECTION
With a little reworking, a vintage factory table can become a wonderfully rustic master-bath vanity. Feet were added to raise the countertop, and the work surface was trimmed to size, with an offcut serving as a backsplash. Drawers were removed to accommodate sinks, then just the fronts were affixed.

CHAPTER 6 >
BATHROOMS

In the hardest-working bathrooms—usually those that are shared—organization is essential. Shaving kits and electric toothbrushes should be handy for the morning rush, for example, with bath salts and fresh towels easily accessible for relaxed evening soaks. A washroom that can handle everything and everyone while remaining uncluttered and retreat-like requires some smart built-in cabinetry and shelving. Consider the clever bath storage ideas on the following pages.

inside

1_ **Vanity Cabinets**

2_ **Wall Storage**

FROM LEFT An oversize vanity means extra interior storage—and a bigger usable countertop. An open shelf offers bonus stowaway space.

For an attic bathroom with a pedestal sink, open cubbies recessed into the eaves can replace lost vanity storage.

Curved feet lighten the look of an unbroken run of cabinetry that includes two sink bases and two banks of drawers.

Vessel sinks—that is, basins that sit above the counter—have a modern look and free up storage space inside the vanity cabinet.

VANITY CABINETS

LIKE SINK BASES IN KITCHENS, vanity cabinets are first and foremost foundations for the business end of indoor plumbing. Yes, there's storage underneath, but once the basin and the pipes are in, there may not be much interior space left—and accessing it requires stooping. As a result, the vanity top actually has the greatest impact on a bathroom's functionality. Make your cabinet between 32 and 43 inches high, depending on what you find comfortable, and plan at least a 36-inch-wide countertop, which yields about 10 inches of workspace on either side of a 16-inch sink. Keep the center of the sink 20 inches from the nearest side-wall, if you can, for comfort. If you're using two vanities or a single one with two sinks—huge improvements for any master bath—make the sinks' center points at least 36 inches apart. The extra elbow room will feel like the ultimate luxury.

HOW TO **CREATE A DRESSER VANITY**

Turning a clothes bureau into a sink cabinet is not as complicated as it may seem. The first step is to pull out the top drawer and detach its front. Then remove the dresser top, unscrewing it from inside the drawer cavity. Rub chalk onto the cut ends of the bathroom pipes, push the dresser against them to mark their locations, and cut out the openings. Add a stone counter with an undermount sink, mount the faucet, and connect the pipes. Attach the tip-out-tray hinges to the drawer front, then to the dresser, and secure the tray. All that is left is to change the pulls and door hinges as desired.

the details

stone sink top

undermount sink

plumbing access holes

new tip-out-tray hinges

tip-out tray

drawer front

new pulls and hinges (optional)

OPPOSITE, CLOCKWISE FROM TOP LEFT

All sorts of furniture pieces can work as vanities, from exotic chests to painted sideboards.

To enhance a vintage dresser's painted finish, distress the edges with sandpaper so the layers of color show through.

When converting an antique, protect its wood top from water damage with cut-to-fit glass or several coats of marine varnish.

The intricate scrollwork on this desk-turned-vanity is made with wood appliqués ordered online and glued in place before painting.

A hand-towel bar mounted on the side prevents drips around the bathroom. ↓

↑DRAWER SMARTS Since the sink gets in the way of having a fully functional top drawer, consider skipping the false front and using full-height doors with easy-to-reach handles. A better place for drawers is alongside the sink, where they offer handy, compartmentalized storage.

TRIM TRICK Always install wall tile before the vanity—that way, there's no need for trimwork to bridge gaps and hide unsightly cut edges, and no worries if you replace your cabinet later on.

↓CLEAN AND SIMPLE Filling a whole wall with base cabinets, an uninterrupted slab of stone, and a framed mirror is the start of a comfortable and sophisticated master-bath layout. Adding more drawers than doors keeps contents better organized.

↑ Glass door panels make it clear where stacks of clean towels reside.

DRESSING ROOM A secretary-style cabinet adds handy shelving, a sit-down workstation, and a little elbow room between his-and-hers vanities.

Open shelving and glass jars put grooming supplies in full view.

119

FROM LEFT A multihued paint scheme brightens this windowless bathroom, and a "halo" shower curtain protects storage cubbies from water.

In a compact bath, take the in-wall design of a medicine cabinet to the next level with an oversize version custom-built for the space.

White paint, glass knobs, and doors that align with the room's wainscoting give a built-in vintage style.

Making this linen cupboard's granite counter higher than the adjoining makeup table gives both the look of freestanding furniture.

WALL STORAGE

FOR BATHROOM SUPPLIES YOU USE EVERY DAY, you want eye-level storage. This can mean anything from the standard mirrored medicine cabinet above the sink to a larger, deeper built-in similar to a hall closet for linens or a pantry for foodstuffs. Kitchen-cabinet companies offer a wide range of modular units that make excellent bathroom pieces. And because they get built in, you can tuck these cabinets into surprisingly tight spots, such as behind the bathroom door, over the sink or toilet, in a small alcove, or even recessed into the wall. Using solid doors will keep less-used (and less-attractive) gear hidden from sight, but a few open shelves or glass panels allow you to create an interesting display with colorful towels or handmade soaps. Be sure to finish cabinets with top-quality mildew-resistant coatings—needed protection in moist environments.

A rollout designed for kitchen garbage works perfectly as a laundry hamper.

↑**EYE-CATCHER** Rich yellow-ochre paint and black strap hinges have a bold visual impact, turning a hutch into the focal point of a family bath.

←STOCK ANSWER
Nearly any bathroom storage need can be accommodated using standard modular base and upper kitchen cabinets.

TRIM TRICK
Stacking base and upper kitchen cabinets is an easy way to create a storage hutch. Topping the base units with painted wood is a thrifty way to create a seamless look. Or use a stone remnant for a luxe accent.

→FOUND SPACE Demolishing an out-of-commission chimney opened up the footprint for this guest-bath recessed shelving unit, highlighted with blue paint and filigreed iron brackets.

Between-the-studs space offers an opportunity for a display niche.

→ DOOR GRILLES
Nodding to the charm of old radiator covers and pie safes, perforated stainless-steel door panels allow air to circulate and damp toiletries to dry.

↑ FLUSH LOOK A vintage-style wood medicine cabinet can be surface mounted or built in. Surface mounting is easier, but recessing the cabinet delivers a neater look and preserves over-the-sink space.

TRIM TRICK Dressing up a plain medicine cabinet with window-like casing details and crown molding makes it feel like a custom-built piece.

→ WALL CUBBY In a bath under a pitched roof, there's often space in the eaves that you can turn into a plentiful storage nook with shelves.

Teak, cedar, and other rot-resistant wood species work as well in baths as they do outdoors. →

INSTALL A MEDICINE CABINET

Medicine cabinets are sold ready to install; you just cut a hole in the wall and create a wood frame to hold it. This Old House technical editor Mark Powers demonstrates how

COST: $200 TO $600

TIME: 4 HOURS

DIFFICULTY: MODERATE

DIY project

TOOLS YOU'LL NEED>
- torpedo level
- drywall keyhole saw
- flashlight
- utility knife
- hacksaw blade
- handsaw
- drywall rasp
- drill/driver
- caulk gun

MATERIALS TO BUY>
- recessed medicine cabinet
- 2×4 One 8-footer
- 1½-inch drywall screws
- 2½-inch deck screws
- construction adhesive
- bathroom caulk

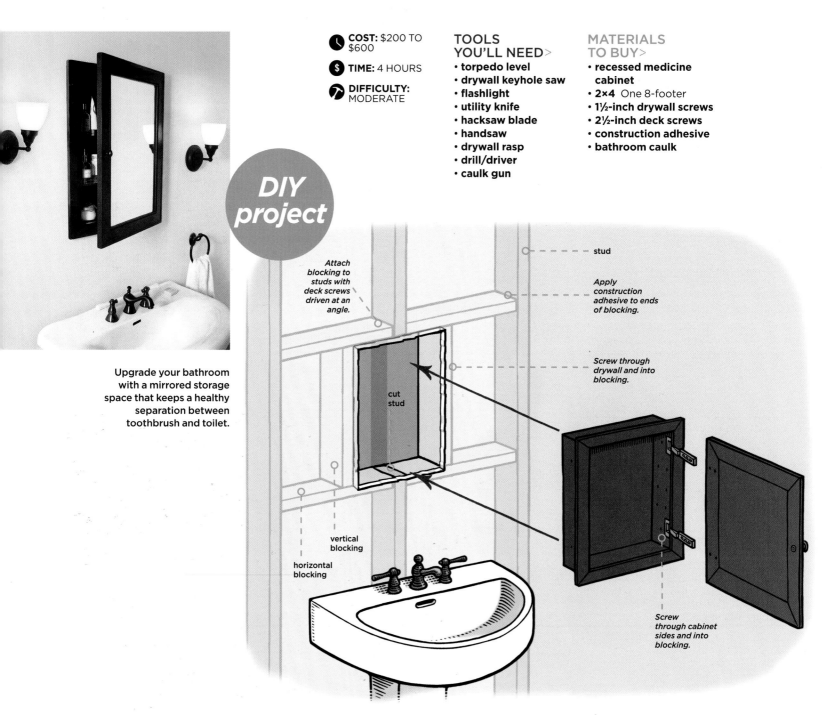

Upgrade your bathroom with a mirrored storage space that keeps a healthy separation between toothbrush and toilet.

Attach blocking to studs with deck screws driven at an angle.

stud

Apply construction adhesive to ends of blocking.

cut stud

Screw through drywall and into blocking.

vertical blocking

horizontal blocking

Screw through cabinet sides and into blocking.

1_ INSPECT THE WALL CAVITY.

Remove the cabinet's mirrored door. Have a helper hold the cabinet against the wall, centering it over the faucet and with the top at 72 inches high. Check the cabinet for plumb and level, and outline its location with a pencil. Using a keyhole saw, open a couple of holes in the drywall within that outline. Angle the saw so that you don't cut beyond the drywall and risk hitting any wires or pipes. Shine a flashlight into the openings and look around for possible obstructions.

2_ CUT THE WALL OPENING.

Contact an electrician and/or a plumber to move wires or pipes, if necessary. Otherwise, use a keyhole saw and a utility knife to cut out the drywall along the penciled outline.

3_ CUT AWAY THE STUD.

There's almost sure to be a stud in the opening. Slide a hacksaw blade, wrapped in tape for a handle, between the stud and the wallboard behind it, and saw through the drywall screws. Then use a handsaw to cut out the stud at the top and the bottom of the wall opening. Test-fit the cabinet, and use a rasp or a utility knife to pare down any tight spots.

4_ INSTALL THE BLOCKING.

Measure horizontally from the intact stud inside the wall to the nearest face of the cut stud. Cut a 2×4 to this length with a handsaw. Repeat three more times until you have four pieces of blocking that fit flush with the top and the bottom of the opening. Dab construction adhesive on the ends, put the pieces of blocking in place, check them for level, and drive drywall screws through the drywall and into the blocking. Then drive pairs of deck screws at an angle through the blocking and into the studs at both ends of each piece. Now measure vertically between the blocking, and cut two more pieces for the vertical sides of the opening. Install in the same manner.

5_ MOUNT THE CABINET.

Insert the cabinet, and drive four drywall screws through the holes in its sides and into the vertical blocking. Caulk the cabinet to the drywall.

6_ REASSEMBLE THE CABINET.

Reattach the cabinet door, making sure not to bend the hinges.

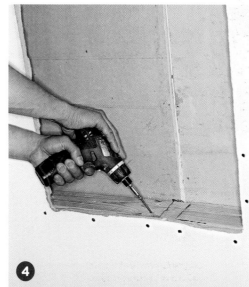

DAYBED FOR NIGHT Most mid-stair landings offer only a place to pivot 180 degrees before continuing the climb. But this bumpout was sized to fit a twin-size daybed that can accommodate sleepover guests.

CHAPTER 7
NOOKS AND NICHES

Every house contains underutilized spaces. Take a look around and you'll start to see them. The end of a hallway, an awkward window alcove, a deep stair landing, odd spots near radiators, and walled-over recesses under the stairs or roof eaves all present wonderful opportunities for built-ins. You can turn these areas into cozy hangouts or highly functional storage holds that hug the margins of your living space. Keep reading for a sampling of clever ideas for forgotten square footage.

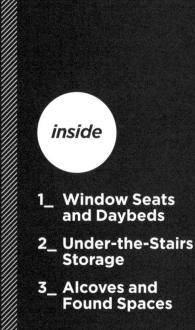

inside

1_ Window Seats and Daybeds

2_ Under-the-Stairs Storage

3_ Alcoves and Found Spaces

FROM LEFT **Paired with a nice, thick cushion, throw pillows can serve as an adjustable backrest to maximize comfort.**

This play-area daybed lives in its own half-walled enclosure, creating a fort-like getaway for kids.

An arched ceiling covered with wood slats shelters this daybed in its own alcove.

A long window seat is an invitation to stretch out and read—or cuddle with a furry friend. Make it fun with bright walls and colorful cushions.

WINDOW SEATS AND DAYBEDS

LIKE FIREPLACES and front porches, there is something about window seats that adds a lot of warmth and charisma to a house. They are the epitome of cozy, often tucked into quirky niches, such as dormers, bays, even turrets. But you can build a window seat (or its mattress-size cousin, the daybed) adjacent to almost any window—or across the room from it, for that matter. If there's a radiator in the way, swap in a toekick heater and add an open grate or screen in front near the floor so that heat can circulate. For forced air, extend the existing ductwork to a grille on the front of the bench box. If storage is needed, add drawers or cabinets to hold closet overflow, or carve out a recess for books. Build your seat 18 inches high, including the cushion, and at least 22 inches deep. Then provide someplace to lean back, and you've got a perfect curl-up spot.

BOOKS AND GAMES
This library shelving incorporates low cabinets with behind-closed-doors storage for board games and sunny seating for perusing books or playing chess or checkers with the kids.

TRIM TRICK
Using a router, you can make attractive, understated slots in the baseboard to act as heating vents.

Beefy exposed hinge barrels with ball tips add drama to simple slab doors.

← BETWEEN CABINETS
This cushioned seat is a clever way to handle a low-lying window in an expansive remodeled kitchen—and makes a restful place to perch while consulting a recipe.

→ POCKET DAYBED
An alcove that is wider than the mattress allows for adding even more practical built-ins: "tables" on either side.

TRIM TRICK
A 4-inch-high platform recessed under a daybed creates a toekick, making it easier to stand close when changing fitted covers or plumping pillows.

HOW TO CREATE A WINDOW SEAT

One shortcut to building a storage bench like this one is to start with stock kitchen cabinets. A lumber platform screwed to the floor raises them up to seat height. Covering the platform with baseboard trim integrates the seat into the surrounding walls. For the U-shaped seat shown here, two double-door cabinets are screwed together through their sides, and a single-door unit forms an L at each end. Filler strips bridge gaps in front, and extra doors act as end panels. The top is supported by cleats mounted to the corners of the walls and is trimmed out with edge molding. A nice, thick cushion makes the seat comfy.

OPPOSITE, CLOCKWISE FROM TOP LEFT

Open cubbies under the seat allow you to store shoes, books, balls, and more, all within arm's reach.

A window seat can house full-size file drawers, plus pullouts in the toekick for oversize items, like wrapping paper.

Create a toasty window seat over a radiator: Lattice panels and open toe space leave outlets for warm air to escape.

Supporting a seat on two end cabinets leaves open stowaway space to park potential trip hazards.

the details

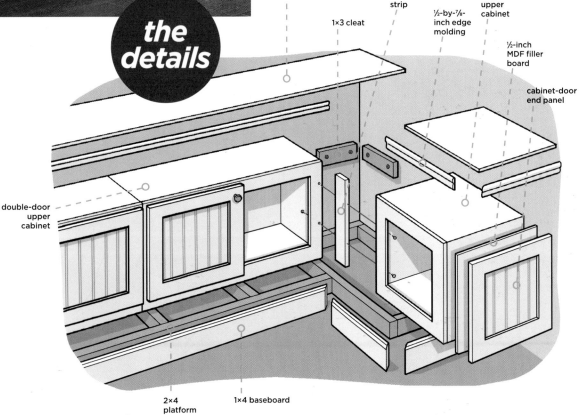

- ¾-inch MDF seat
- 1×3 cleat
- 1×2 filler strip
- ½-by-⅞-inch edge molding
- single-door upper cabinet
- ½-inch MDF filler board
- cabinet-door end panel
- double-door upper cabinet
- 2×4 platform
- 1×4 baseboard

→**FOLD-OUT BED** This is one of a pair of family-room perches that flanks a built-in media cabinet. By day, it has top-floor views of the tree-lined neighborhood. But for sleepovers, the custom one-piece seat top and front lifts up, and a standard sofa-bed mechanism and mattress pull out.

Built-in sofas

The most comfortable perches share one thing in common—cushioning to sit on and lean against. In living rooms and family spaces where square footage is tight, a built-in sofa with a fully cushioned seat and back can be a smart solution. It can even boost storage, if that's part of the overall design. The back can be made like an upholstered headboard and fastened in place, but zippered, loose cushions held to the frame with heavy-duty Velcro are easily detachable and make cleaning easier. You can make the cushions yourself, have them produced by a local upholstery shop, or even order them custom-sewn from an online retailer. Just make sure to use a high-grade upholstery fabric for durability.

1_ SHAPED BY CABINETS Columns of open shelving with deep file-cabinet bases create a surround for this built-in sofa. Walnut cabinet tops double as end tables.

2_ BACKED BY SHELVING Symmetrical lines give a traditional look to this combination of shelves and seating.

3_ FLANKED ON EITHER END An upholstered back, a contoured seat cushion, and a pleated skirt give this seat—boxed in on both sides—the formality of a full-fledged couch.

FROM LEFT Four kids make use of this tucked-away basement printer station via wireless connections.

Even if you can't build beneath the stairway, putting cabinets alongside it still maximizes space since little else could fit so perfectly.

Specially outfitted for glassware and table linens, these pullouts work like a dining room sideboard that frees up the floor.

Rope lighting brightens living-room recessed shelves used for oversize books and decorative accents.

UNDER-THE-STAIRS STORAGE

IF YOU HAVE NO BASEMENT—or its access is located elsewhere—the space under your main stairway can serve all sorts of handy purposes. Sometimes a half bath is even squeezed in there. But where the ceiling would be too steeply sloped for such a use, building in storage can make the most of the space without requiring that anyone stoop to enter. Under-the-stairs cabinets can stow anything from shoes to wine to outerwear. In a formal foyer, putting a coat cabinet behind these doors hides any mess that may accumulate inside. In casual areas, open cubbies may be handier to use or offer spots to put collectibles on display. And even if there is no room under the stairs, building cabinetry alongside them is still a space-conserving way to organize and declutter your home.

→HIDDEN ASSET A secret compartment under a front-hall stair landing conceals a coat closet. Matching picture-frame paneling blends the doors into the rest of the wall.

←STAIR CUBBIES Running the treads and risers past the stringers—the notched pieces that support a stair—creates a large shoe rack conveniently located by a well-used entry door. Be sure to consult your municipal building department to ensure that any stair design meets local code.

WINE PULLOUT Built using sturdy full-extension cabinet slides, this 32-bottle rack takes advantage of unused under-stair space.

TRIM TRICK
To make hidden storage blend into a paneled wall, build the cabinets, drawers, or doors first, then attach a section of paneling that has been cut to align perfectly with the surrounding pattern.

With the rack fully pulled out, each row slides forward for bottle access.

141

Holes in the sides fit pins that allow shelves to adjust as needs change.

←**WEDGE DRESSER** Deep drawers tucked into the void behind the steps can be built just like old furniture, with boxes that ride on waxed wood guides.

TRIM TRICK

There's no need to build angled drawers. Just put angled fronts on standard rectangular boxes to fool the eye. Paint-to-match knobs are easy to grasp but recede visually.

←**STEPPED DOWN**
Bookshelf units of descending height capitalize on the angled wall along a basement staircase.

→**CLEVER CAMOUFLAGE** A full-height closet takes advantage of the space under a wide stair landing—and under the stairs themselves, now the closet's access point.

Wood turn latches hold the space-saving bifold doors in place when closed.

FROM LEFT Home centers and online suppliers sell classic display niches as one-piece units that are easy to install between wall studs.

Chest-high cabinets provide storage for linens and extra toiletries while adding a visual anchor at the quiet end of an upstairs hallway.

This hideaway cabinet in a short passageway between two rooms gives the phrase "pocket door" new meaning.

A top-of-the-stairs built-in with triangular recessed shelves proffers a subliminal invitation to visit the finished attic.

ALCOVES AND FOUND SPACES

{ **SOMETIMES YOU CAN** add storage, seating, or other useful built-ins without giving up a single square inch of functional floor space. Recessed into the wall or a tight corner where nobody ever steps foot, these can be showy feats of carpentry, like a well-proportioned bookshelf calling attention to the lonely end of a hall. Or they can blend into their surroundings, such as an in-wall shelving unit with a door that precisely matches the paneling all around it, with hidden hinges and push latches to make sure nobody would ever know that the cabinet is even there. Either way, thanks to their ability to shrink themselves into forgotten corners—or even duck inside the walls—these clever alcove built-ins make your house feel bigger than it actually is because you're getting more mileage out of the footprint that's already there.

Coated with chalkboard paint, the back panel handles reminders, lists, and kids' doodles.

↑**MESSAGE CENTER**
Taking advantage of the space between wall studs, this cabinet puts a family bulletin board in a convenient kitchen spot but hides any mess when the door is closed.

↓**IN-WALL BOOKCASE** An open stairway requires a safety rail. Make it a low wall and thicken it to 9 inches deep, and you can also put in shelving to hold books, games, or toys.

LANDING NOOK A recessed mudroom bench beside the stairs to the garage yields a spot to sit and pull on boots—and to drop off groceries coming in from the car.

TRIM TRICK
Painting the walls, trim, and alcove all one color creates a cohesive look that visually tidies up an open storage space.

← AROUND A DOOR

Instead of trying to hide a garage door that opens directly into a family room, define it: Add a surround of black-painted shelves to form a decorative nook for books and knickknacks.

TRIM TRICK

Backing open shelves with beadboard, either plywood or MDF, is an easy way to dress them up—and you can hide horizontal seams behind the boards.

↑ MAGAZINE RACK A modified cabinet end between the sitting area and the master suite offers angled slots for storing and organizing reading materials.

← SUPPLY STASH

Top-of-the-stairs shelves with a handsome face frame offer a convenient spot for storing backup bulk goods between the kitchen and the basement.

↑**SECRET ROOM** Dead space behind the wall of a first-floor powder room inspired a hidden storage area for overflow sporting equipment and cleaning supplies.

TRIM TRICK

To create a false-front cabinet like this, apply all the parts—face frame, drawer fronts, and moldings—to a plywood backer that's hung like a door.

↑ The closet door features two real cubbies and six fixed drawer fronts.

Knee-wall storage

In houses with finished attics, or eaves that continue down over other living spaces, it's common to find knee walls, which are short partitions tucked under the rafters. These help to define the rooms and prevent the sloping ceiling from continuing all the way to the floor, where no person, furniture, or even vacuum attachment could ever fit. Still, the void behind a knee wall can accommodate any number of built-ins, from open shelving to dresser drawers to closed cabinets. Just what will fit inside the space is only a matter of its height and depth.

1_ CLOTHES DRESSER
Where the space behind a knee wall is not quite deep enough, bumping in the whole wall can make room for a full-size chest of built-in drawers.

2_ MEDIA CABINET
A mix of open and closed storage in the wall opposite the bed in an attic master suite handsomely houses the TV, its components, and other necessities.

3_ OFFICE-SUPPLY SHELVES In a compact attic workspace, high knee walls provide ample space for deep shelving to store files and office gear.

OFF THE KITCHEN
Plan a gap for legroom between a pair of base cabinets, and the countertop can become a useful computer station connected to the action in the cook space.

CHAPTER 8 >
OFFICE AREAS

Whether you're creating a formal library with a banker's desk and bookshelves lining the walls or planning a laptop nook in the kitchen or the family room to keep an eye on kids surfing the Internet, built-ins are key to fitting in a just-right desk and storage area. You can use stock cabinetry and a laminate countertop or custom woodwork and a stone slab to create your workspace. Check out the smart solutions on the following pages.

inside

FROM LEFT White-washed maple cabinets store paperwork and desk supplies, while a one-piece concrete slab provides the desktop.

Cherry built-ins give this home office a library look. A shallow cabinet in the kneehole hides cords and cables behind doors.

A wood top makes an ideal desk surface, while sunny yellow paint on all the built-ins energizes this office space.

Folding French doors segregate this airy home office from the main living space when it's time to focus.

WORK-AT-HOME OFFICES

{ **E-MAIL AND THE INTERNET** made it possible. Gas prices and tight corporate budgets made it happen—at least for some. Today, one in four workers, including part-timers and the self-employed, does at least some of his or her job from home. It's a great way to balance career and family responsibilities and to eliminate the commute. But to make it work—and to qualify for that desirable home-office tax deduction—there is one absolute necessity: a truly separate area, where you can get away from the noises and distractions of the household. So wherever your workspace is located—a converted attic, a finished basement, a spare bedroom, or a loft over the garage—in addition to shelving, a desk, and a dedicated phone line, you need a door you can shut tight.

Eyesores like the printer and the shredder hide inside cabinet pullouts.

ONE CHAIR, TWO DESKS A mahogany writing table is set up to receive clients with a computer workstation just a swivel of the desk chair away. Additional work surfaces, storage cabinets, and shelves are positioned around the room's perimeter.

Desk guidelines

Anyone who spends considerable time working at a computer station needs to take precautions to avoid repetitive stress injury and eyestrain. Here's how to create an ergonomic setup that maximizes both function and comfort.

Distance from monitor to user: an arm's length away, with the top of the screen slightly below eye level

Desktop width: at least 30 inches

Desktop depth: at least 19 inches

Desktop height: 28 inches

Seat height: 14½ to 18½ inches; feet should be flat, knees level with hips, forearms parallel to the floor, elbows bent at 90 degrees, and wrists straight or flexed down when typing.

※

TOH DESIGN ADVICE

A standard desk is usually too high for proper hand position when typing, so plan to mount a rollout keyboard tray under the desktop to get your setup right.

→ON DISPLAY
Located in a living room alcove, this landscape architect's desktop is made of plywood wrapped in stainless steel and supported with chunky wood brackets. Wraparound floating shelves put office supplies and reference books within arm's reach. Chalkboard paint over three layers of magnetic paint turns the back wall into a bulletin board and message center.

Behind the lower door is a printer on a rollout shelf and a pair of file drawers.

→NOTCHED FOR COMFORT A cutout in the desktop ensures that the user can sit appropriately close to the screen, while having papers and the printer within easy reach.

Heavy-duty hardware allows extra-deep file drawers to fully extend. →

FROM LEFT This simple desk area, made from kitchen cabinets, hosts a pass-through that also provides a view.

Wired for a TV, smartphone chargers, and a laptop plug, a hutch-style office doubles as a media center.

Opening away from the food-prep area, this end cabinet houses a corkboard and a pair of electrical outlets.

This desk between the kitchen and the mudroom gets its handsome look from clear-finished oak, black granite, and an old-school phone.

KITCHEN OFFICES

YOU DO FAR MORE than cook and eat in the kitchen. It is the house's natural social center—and a handy place to pay bills, set up schedules, and keep connected with the world. Those activities call for a dedicated space near the cooking area but outside the main thoroughfares, where you can sit to use a PC, laptop, or tablet or occasionally even put pen to paper. The simplest solution is an opening under a stretch of countertop that's at least 30 inches wide, with a chair and an outlet to charge wireless devices. But you can also hang a bulletin-board backsplash, devote a base cabinet or two to storing files and a printer, and stow office supplies in an upper cabinet. With a connected kitchen, you'll see those last-minute e-mails from guests even as you're prepping the party meal.

→ OFFICE ALCOVE
Built into a recess where a chimney once stood, this work area has a special ceiling treatment that makes it feel like a distinct space on a fully open main floor.

↑ CLASSIC BEAUTY It looks like a freestanding piece, but this custom-built tiger-maple secretary with a fold-down desktop is anchored to the wall like the rest of the kitchen cabinetry.

TRIM TRICK

Keeping a built-in's crown molding lower than the ceiling's crown simplifies installation since you don't have to marry the trim to the molding that's already in place.

→ MULTIFUNCTION AREA With a laptop open, it's a spot to check messages while cooking, but take away the computer and it becomes a bar, with glassware and liquor stashed in the surrounding cabinets.

An opening in a side cabinet is a convenient place to stash the printer.
↓

Electric, phone, and Ethernet jacks offer connection to the outside world.
↓

↑**KITCHEN CORNER** A sit-down desk situated outside of the hustle and bustle of the work triangle offers a calm spot for paying bills and checking e-mail.

← OPENED UP
Near a casual kitchen's sliding door to the deck, cubbies and shelves keep office gear sorted and connect visually to the divided-light transom window.

↑
A perforated-metal panel hides the computer and vents the heat that it generates.

→ STAND-UP STATION
This seatless command center accommodates tasks like scribbling calendar commitments and setting up lunch dates before you head off to work or between errands.

TRIM TRICK
Though the arched center cubby looks impressive, making it can be as simple as cutting a curve in the face frame's upper rail.

FROM LEFT Tucked into a corridor off the kitchen, this desk's flipper doors slide out and swing closed to hide the paper that inevitably piles up.

Under a library ladder for accessing 10-foot-high kitchen cabinets, this computer also works as a TV and controls the whole-house audio system.

These homework stations were inspired by library carrels. The upper cabinets hold school and art supplies and hide ductwork.

Make a built-in kid's desk full-size and just use different-height chairs as she grows.

MORE BUILT-IN DESKS

THANKS TO EVER-TINIER LAPTOPS—not to mention electronic bill paying and digital calendars—you can fit everything you need for a functional household office into a small cupboard, hutch, or closet. That is a boon to anyone looking to add a desk area to a house without much room to spare. You can put an amazingly functional workspace into a closet simply by setting the lowest shelf at desk height, about 28 inches, and providing space for a chair to fit when the seat is tucked under the desktop and the door is closed. Or use a fold-down desktop, retractable cabinet doors, or a wall of cabinetry to create a desk area in the middle of the family room or the master suite that can close up and disappear from view when it's not in use.

Window treatments are a must to block glare on any desktop where you might use a computer. →

ATTIC OFFICE At its very simplest, a desk can be just a sturdy shelf hung in a natural alcove of the house.

TRIM TRICK

To install a shelf desk made from a solid door slab, first screw wood strips, or cleats, into the studs in all the surrounding walls, then attach the desktop to those supports.

← FOLDAWAY DESK
The desk and lower shelf disappear into the wall, thanks to a hinged desktop and cabinet doors that double as its supports.

→ CRAFTS AND COMPUTER
An expansive L-shaped office built-in keeps paint and crafting supplies well sorted and accessible. Wide flipper doors close off the entire desktop when not in use, putting work out of sight.

Control clutter by stashing stationery and supplies in labeled, stackable boxes.

↓

↑CLOSET CONVERSION When space is tight, a home office may seem like a luxury, but you can carve one out of a seldom-used closet by removing the existing rod and adding shelves and an electrical outlet. Bifold doors make the nook look wide-open and welcoming.

→PANTRY OFFICE
Converting a butler's pantry into a home office provides a footprint large enough for abundant storage; the contrasting citrusy color scheme of this office gives it a distinct identity.

→CABINET INSET
Much like a kitchen desk, this living-room computer station consists of a gap in the wall of built-ins, both over and under the countertop. Surrounded by lots of uncluttered display space, the screen does not detract from the overall decor.

A bar-height desk helps the user feel like part of the kitchen action.

A FRESH SPIN To-the-ceiling cabinets with a rolling library ladder, quartzite counters, mosaic tile, and a sink window trimmed with leftover stone make this laundry space as pleasant as it is functional.

CHAPTER 9 >
EVERYDAY NECESSITIES

Some of the most beneficial built-ins are designed for the humdrum, taken-for-granted routines of daily life. No cabinets can fold the mountains of laundry that a young family creates, of course, or walk the dog on a blustery winter night, but they can organize the supplies needed for those jobs—and help create an attractive, efficient, and inviting place to spend time in. On the pages that follow, see how well-thought-out built-ins can simplify laundry and pet-keeping chores.

inside

1_ **Laundry Areas**

2_ **Pet Solutions**

FROM LEFT A stone countertop with turned-leg supports offers unfettered access to a pair of front-loading machines.

Open shelves with curved brackets, plank wainscoting, and a soapstone counter blend time-honored looks with totally modern function.

Clean and classic, this laundry room–pantry features an apron sink and granite counters made from a bargain remnant.

Embrace the opportunity to wake up a laundry space with bright colors and fun accents that you might not dare to use elsewhere.

LAUNDRY AREAS

THE SIMPLE FACT IS that your washer and dryer don't belong in the basement. Hiking down a flight or two of stairs with every dirty load and then back up with every clean one is back-wrenching work that inevitably means scraping knuckles on doorjambs and dropping just-cleaned items on the dusty cellar floor. Even if a full-scale laundry room—with cabinets, countertop, drying rack, and sink—is not feasible in your house, consider moving the machines to the main bedroom floor, where most of the dirty laundry collects. Or put the washer and dryer in a first-floor mudroom, another magnet for soiled gear. A storage cubby or two and a sturdy countertop will add a convenient place to fold and sort.

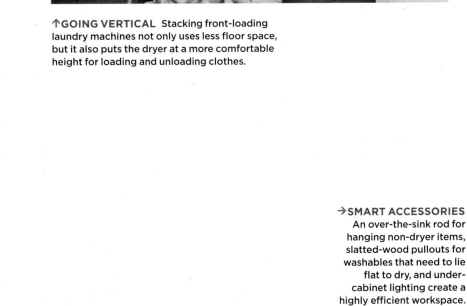

↑**GOING VERTICAL** Stacking front-loading laundry machines not only uses less floor space, but it also puts the dryer at a more comfortable height for loading and unloading clothes.

→**BACK-HALL LAUNDRY**
A laundry area with a sink makes an excellent addition to a mudroom, since that's where the wettest and muddiest clothes get stripped off. A one-piece stone counter makes a splashproof sink surround and an easy-to-wipe-down folding surface.

TRIM TRICK
Installing sheets of beadboard as wainscoting and a backsplash is an easy way to tie beadboard-panel cabinet doors into the room as a whole.

→**SMART ACCESSORIES**
An over-the-sink rod for hanging non-dryer items, slatted-wood pullouts for washables that need to lie flat to dry, and under-cabinet lighting create a highly efficient workspace.

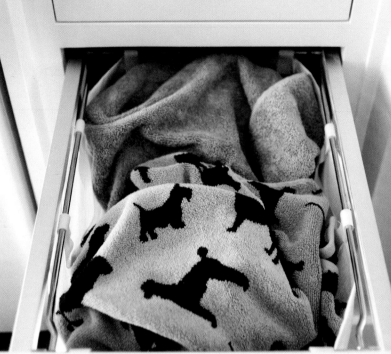

Laundry cabinet guidelines

To put your front-loading washer and dryer into cabinets or a closet, you'll need to allow proper clearances for the plumbing, electrical, and venting. Follow these general measurements along with those listed in your machines' manuals.

OPPOSITE, CLOCKWISE FROM TOP LEFT

Tuck a musty towel into this top-floor chute, and it falls all the way to the basement laundry area—eliminating the need to haul dirties downstairs.

A full-height cabinet drawer lined with a removable canvas hamper bag gives family members a spot to dump soiled clothing.

A laundry-room island offers a handy folding surface—and can provide cubby space for individual laundry baskets designated for different load types.

A pop-out ironing-board kit that you can retrofit into an existing drawer keeps this sometimes unwieldy accessory neatly tucked away.

Cabinet depth: at least 38 inches to accommodate pipes, wiring, and venting

Cabinet interior width: at least 29 inches per machine

Bottom of countertop to floor: at least 38 inches, or full height of machine, with no moldings or obstructions to interfere with removal

✳ TOH DESIGN ADVICE

Be sure to insulate the back wall of a laundry cabinet to reduce sound transfer, put rubber anti-vibration pads under the machines (factor in an additional inch of countertop height), and install a drain pan in the floor to catch any leaks.

FROM LEFT A tall rollout cabinet designed for garbage and recycling makes a perfect storage spot for bulk pet provisions.

This floor-level island cubby gives Fido a cave-like hangout near his family, so he's not lying underfoot.

A custom stainless-steel liner protects this open cabinet from water and food spills, a given at doggie dinnertime.

Made with furniture-grade materials and a vent-grille door panel, this end table doubles as a dog crate.

PET SOLUTIONS

{ **THE FAMILY DOG—OR CAT—**comes with a lot of paraphernalia, from mealtime supplies (often bought in bulk) to grooming tools to chew toys. With a little planning, you can build cabinets to handle all that and more, keeping it accessible but out of the way. That means you'll never again have to search for the claw clippers, stumble over the water bowl, or relocate a bed that keeps drifting across the floor. You can organize the accoutrements of pet ownership with a rollout tray for vat-sized containers of kibble or a waterproof recess that holds food and water dishes. Or build yourself a wall-hung organizer for all that dog-walking stuff—including the leash that matches your mutt's collar and the tennis-ball launcher that starts his tail wagging as soon as you pick it up.

↑CAT CABINET Simply removing a laundry-room cabinet-door panel and replacing it with curtains gives the family feline an out-of-the-way spot for a plush bed, food and water bowls, or a litter box.

→ CANINE BED
A simple wood frame lined with a firm foam cushion (and a washable cover) gives this pooch a built-in bed of his own, right in the mudroom.

→ SLIDE-OUT SUPPER
A drawer built into the island toekick and fitted with a pair of pet bowls pulls out when needed and pushes in again when company calls.

TRIM TRICK
Drawer glides aren't necessary here. Just apply self-stick felt pads to the bottom of the box, and it will slide smoothly over the floor.

Wire-mesh door panels provide needed ventilation. →

← UNDER-SINK CABINET
This cat-shaped entry was cut with a jigsaw to provide access to the litter box inside. The bottomless cabinet sits on the pantry's scratchproof and easy-to-clean concrete floor.

TRIM TRICK

To cut out a symmetrical design like this one, stack the doors back-to-back, and clamp them together. Mark one-half of the desired outline, and then cut both doors at once.

← HANDSOME HANGOUT You can easily modify any bookcase that is at least 15 inches deep to accommodate furry friends. Pull out the lower shelves, add pillows, and secure it to the wall if it is freestanding.

TRIM TRICK

To turn a stained wood cabinet into an open cubby, unscrew the hinges to remove the doors and fill the holes with wood putty that's in the closest possible color match.

→ KITCHEN CUBBY
For pets who are being crate-trained, a custom base cabinet can get the metal cage out of the middle of the room—and Rover can still be part of the kitchen action.

BUILD A WALL-MOUNTED PET ORGANIZER

Make yourself a spot to stow toys, treats, and gear for your pooch's daily walks, and you'll never have to hunt down these items again. TOH technical editor Mark Powers runs through the step-by-step

$ COST: $60

⏱ TIME: 5 HOURS

⚙ DIFFICULTY: MODERATE

TOOLS YOU'LL NEED>

- circular saw
- compound miter saw
- pin nailer
- caulk gun
- clamps
- work gloves
- tin snips
- drill/driver
- paintbrushes

MATERIALS TO BUY>

- **½-inch plywood beadboard** One 4-by-4-foot sheet
- **1×6 trim** One 6-footer
- **1×5 trim** One 3-footer
- **⁹⁄₁₆-by-1⅝-inch bed molding** One 3-footer
- **¹¹⁄₁₆-by-1⅛-inch backband molding** One 8-footer
- **¼-by-¾-inch edge molding** One 3-footer
- **¼-inch square dowel** One 3-footer
- **⅝-inch square dowel** One 2-footer
- **½- and 1-inch 23-gauge nails**
- **½-inch sheet-metal screws**
- **¾- and 1-inch wood screws**
- **3-inch deck screws**
- **⅜-inch hole plugs**
- **18½-by-13-inch metal ceiling tile**
- **hooks**
- **carpenter's glue**
- **adhesive caulk**
- **150-grit sandpaper**
- **primer** and **paint**

This simple wall unit stows everything needed for a morning walk, from the leash to plastic bags.

DIY project

Finished dimensions: 25"W × 4½"D × 34"H

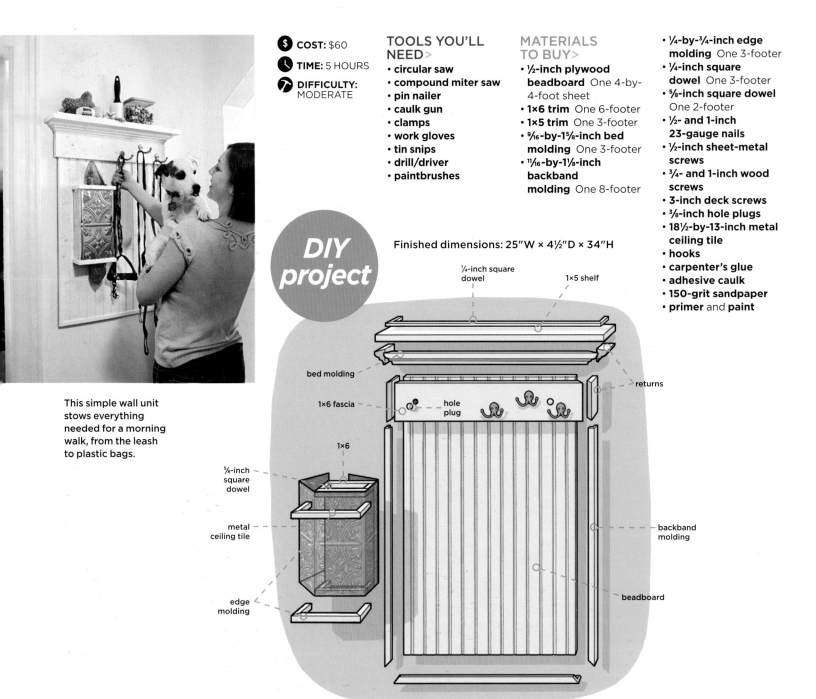

¼-inch square dowel · 1×5 shelf · bed molding · 1×6 fascia · hole plug · returns · ⅝-inch square dowel · metal ceiling tile · 1×6 · edge molding · backband molding · beadboard

1_ ASSEMBLE THE BEADBOARD AND FASCIA.
Use a circular saw to cut the beadboard to size: 21 by 33 inches. Use a compound miter saw to cut 45-degree outside miters onto the 1×6 fascia; its point-to-point length should be 22½ inches. Next, use the miter saw to cut two 1¼-inch-long mitered returns from scrap 1×6. Fasten to the fascia with carpenter's glue and 1-inch nails, then glue and nail the fascia to the beadboard so that the top edges are flush with each other.

2_ ATTACH THE SHELF AND MOLDING.
Cut the 1×5 shelf to length: 25 inches. Squeeze adhesive caulk along the fascia's top edge, then set the shelf so it's centered from side to side and flush with the beadboard's back face. Fasten it by shooting 1-inch nails through the shelf and into the fascia's top edge. Round over the shelf's front corners with sandpaper. Miter-cut the bed molding to 23⅝ inches, then make returns long enough to meet the wall. Attach the molding to the fascia and shelf with glue and 1-inch nails.

3_ ADD THE RAIL AND BACKBAND.
Cut to length three ¼-inch square dowels with outside miters to be installed ¼ inch from the shelf's edges; secure with glue and ½-inch nails. Cut three lengths of backband molding to fit around the beadboard's edges, mitering the bottom corners. Secure with caulk and ½-inch nails.

4_ MAKE THE BAG DISPENSER.
To make this open-ended box, glue four ⅝-inch square dowels, each two inches long, upright onto the corners of a 13-inch-long 1×6. Then glue two 5½-inch-long dowels atop the short ones to form two rectangular frames. Clamp until dry. Wearing gloves, cut a ceiling tile to size with tin snips. Place the tile on the edge of a work surface, make four bends, and wrap around the frame. Fasten the ends to the 1×6's back with sheet-metal screws. Cover exposed metal edges with edge molding, cut to length and mitered for outside corners; secure with caulk and ½-inch nails. Sand, prime, and paint all exposed wood.

5_ ATTACH THE DISPENSER.
Apply caulk to the back of the dispenser, set it in place on the beadboard, and drive 1-inch wood screws through the back of the beadboard into the back of the dispenser.

6_ MOUNT THE HOOKS AND THE ORGANIZER.
Position the hooks, drill 1/16-inch pilot holes, and attach with ¾-inch screws. Mount the organizer to the studs with deck screws, and cover their heads with plugs.

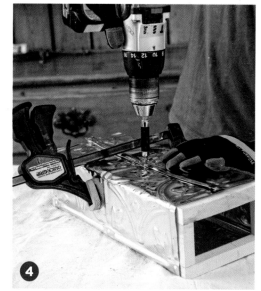

CHAPTER 10 >
BEDROOMS

They may be the last places you think of when it comes to adding built-ins. After all, bedrooms aren't generally spots where guests will see and admire the craftsmanship of custom cabinetry. Nor are they hubs of overlapping activities and abundant gear—the way kitchens and mudrooms are—where the need for hardworking storage is unmistakable. Still, built-ins can declutter and organize a family's personal spaces, creating a calm and peaceful environment for those precious, restful hours of the day. Keep reading for ingenious ways to maximize space in your bedrooms.

inside

FROM LEFT Head-to-head beds with slide-out trundles for sleepovers create a cozy bedtime environment.

A built-in bed under a sloped ceiling, with the foot under the low point, makes the most of limited attic space.

Raising youngsters' beds loft-style allows for kid-sized closets underneath.

With an arched and paneled alcove frame and a nautically themed wall mural, this bed feels as snug as a ship's berth.

BUILT-IN BEDS

MOST FREESTANDING BEDS look far better on the showroom floor than they prove to be when you get them home. Maybe they're just too bulky for a room's compact space, the footboard blocks the view of the master-suite TV, the bed frame creaks annoyingly when you move, or the finish shows every tiny ding and scrape. So when the time comes to spring for an upgrade, forget the usual mass-produced furniture options. A built-in bed will deliver a custom fit for any particular space's footprint, scale, and decor. And it can boost bedroom storage with drawers and cubbies in the usually overlooked space under and around the mattress. Whether it's a king-size master-suite sleeper, a set of bunks for the kids, or a spare bed for guests, durable custom carpentry typically costs no more than what you would spend on high-end store-bought furniture.

↑HIDE-A-BED A fold-down Murphy bed anchored to the wall offers comfortable accommodations in a guest suite. It tips up into a wood frame—lined with upholstery fabric for a headboard effect—and disappears behind curtains when not in use.

→TIGHT QUARTERS Two sets of head-to-head kids' beds fit nicely along a narrow attic space. Stacked rows of open and closed storage under the platforms replace a dresser for each child.

→SNUG FIT This basement guest room's bed not only has drawer storage below but also has a headboard thick enough to function as a bookshelf and an end table. Since there is no side rail, making up and changing linens is easy.

TRIM TRICK
For a shortcut to creating paneled wainscot, apply a framework of ½-inch lattice strips directly over the drywall, and top with a chair rail.

Operable porthole windows allow siblings to open them up for a chat.
↓

→**SHIPSHAPE** Built-in bunks—twin-size on the top and full on the bottom—were designed with a staircase at the end containing a dresser drawer in each riser, plus an inset book cubby for the lower bed.

TRIM TRICK
Routing simple V-grooves into the treads of built-in bunk-bed stairs will improve traction for little feet.

Bunk-bed safety

Stacking kids' beds saves space in small rooms, and children love their cozy confines. To make them safe, however, requires strong and stable bases for the mattresses and a properly designed railing up top. Rails should wrap around all open sides of the upper bed (as well as the bottom one if it's more than 30 inches off the ground), stand at least 5 inches higher than the top of the mattress, and have a single opening at one end, no larger than 15 inches wide, for ladder access. For other specs, consult an experienced furniture maker, or go to the Consumer Products Safety Commission website. And remember to limit top-bunk use to kids ages 6 and up.

1_ SOLID SIDE
A sturdy wall of plywood ensures that no child or stuffed animal will fall through.

2_ OPEN STYLE
Slatted railings should be correctly spaced to eliminate any risk of a child passing through or getting a limb caught.

3_ SEE-THROUGH
Panels made of clear acrylic sheeting create a gap-free barrier that still allows children to see what's going on down below.

DIY project

In addition to sleek lines, classic beadboard panels, and Victorian rosette details, this bed includes seven handy storage cubbies.

BUILD A STORAGE BED

Why spend thousands on a mass-produced piece? On the following pages, This Old House contributor Christopher Beidel shows you how to custom-build a bed that's as practical as it is handsome

$ COST: $350, PLUS A QUEEN-SIZE MATTRESS

🕐 TIME: 10–12 HOURS

📐 DIFFICULTY: MODERATE

Finished dimensions: 64½"W × 83½"L × 21¼"H (suitable for a queen-size mattress)

TOOLS YOU'LL NEED>
- **long bar clamps**
- **straightedge**
- **circular saw**
- **drill/driver** or **impact driver**
- **paintbrushes** and **roller**
- **brad nailer**
- **miter saw**
- **jigsaw** or **Japanese handsaw**
- **caulk gun**

MATERIALS TO BUY>
- **¾-inch medium-density fiberboard (MDF)** Five 4-by-8-foot sheets
- **⅜-inch MDF beadboard panels** Two 4-by-8 sheets
- **1×2 MDF trim** Eleven 8-footers, primed
- **2×4s** Three 8-footers
- **Victorian-era door casing kit (includes rosettes)**
- **½×3 lattice strip** One 4-footer
- **¾-inch quarter-round molding** Three 8-footers
- **1¼-, 1½-, and 2-inch MDF screws**
- **2½-inch deck screws**
- **1- and 1¼-inch 18-gauge nails**
- **carpenter's glue**
- **construction adhesive**
- **150-grit sandpaper**
- **primer** and **paint**
- **wood filler**

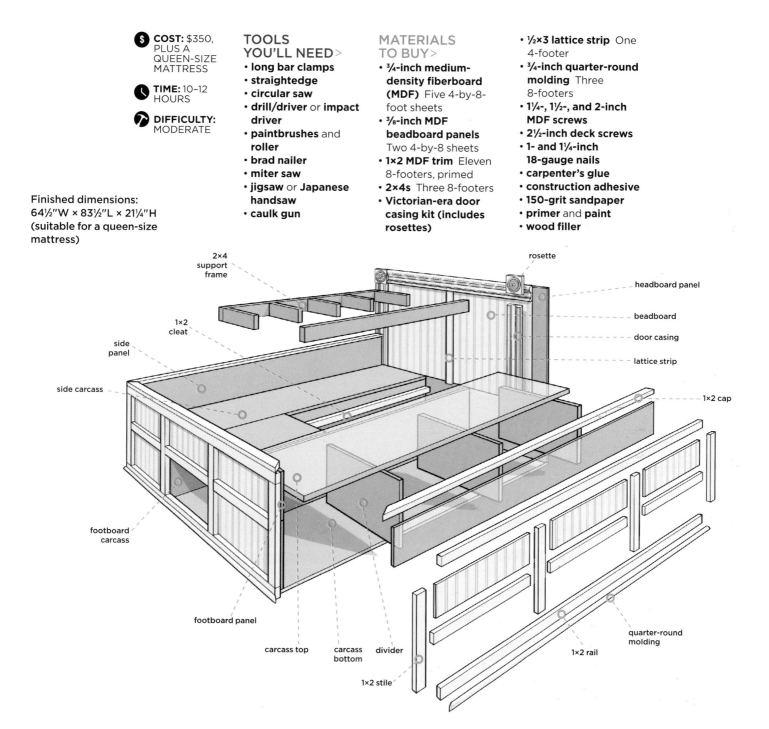

2×4 support frame
1×2 cleat
side panel
side carcass
footboard carcass
footboard panel
carcass top
carcass bottom
divider
1×2 stile
1×2 rail
quarter-round molding
1×2 cap
lattice strip
door casing
beadboard
headboard panel
rosette

1_ CUT THE MDF SHEETS.

The mattress platform is made up of three storage carcasses: one on each side with three bays, and a one-bay box that fits between those two, at the foot. Clamp a straightedge in place and use a circular saw to cut the pieces for the side carcasses: two tops and two bottoms at 21 by 82 inches, two backs at 10½ by 82 inches, and eight dividers at 10½ by 20¼ inches. For the foot carcass, cut a top and a bottom piece at 21 by 27½ inches each, two side pieces at 10½ by 26¾ inches, and a back piece at 10½ by 21 inches.

2_ ASSEMBLE THE CARCASSES.

Lay flat the bottom piece for a side carcass, and run a bead of carpenter's glue atop its back edge. Stand the back piece on edge on the glue line and use four bar clamps to hold it upright. Then get a partner to help tip up the L-shaped assembly, and drill pilot holes through the bottom and into the edge. Screw the pieces together with 1½-inch MDF screws. Evenly space the four dividers along the length of the carcass, and glue, clamp, and screw them in place. Do the same for the top piece. Build the other two carcasses in the same way.

3_ DRY-FIT THE CARCASSES.

Arrange the three carcasses as they will be assembled, and clamp them together at the foot. Measure the length and width of the void between them, as shown. Prime all surfaces.

4_ JOIN THE CARCASSES. Grab a

partner and move the carcasses into the bedroom. Place them on 1×2 furring strips so that the bottom rails will be flush with the storage openings, then clamp them back together. Use 1¼-inch MDF screws to fasten the sides of the small carcass to the adjacent ones.

5_ INSTALL THE SUPPORT FRAME.

Fill the void in the platform with a frame made of 2×4s cut to length: two at 54½ inches and five at 18 inches. Drive deck screws through the long boards into the ends of the five crosspieces. Install 1×2 MDF cleats around the platform opening, 3½ inches down from the top. These will hold the frame flush with the platform. Set the frame on the cleats and fasten it to the carcasses using 2-inch MDF screws.

6_ CUT THE BED-FRAME PIECES. Use

a straightedge and a circular saw to cut the two 8½-by-82-inch MDF side panels and 8½-by-61½-inch footboard panel. The sides will overlap the footboard panel and butt into the headboard panel.

7_ INSTALL THE SIDE PANELS. Run a bead of glue along the perimeter of the platform, one side at a time. Place each panel on edge in the glue and clamp it in place. Check that it is square and flush with the platform. Drill pilot holes up into the edges of the panels through the storage bays, and into the edges of the footboard panel through the side panels. Drive 1½-inch MDF screws into each hole.

8_ INSTALL THE HEADBOARD. Cut the MDF headboard panel to size: 18 by 63 inches. Use 1¼-inch MDF screws to attach it to the carcasses and the 2×4 frame. Don't use glue if you ever plan to move the bed.

9_ INSTALL THE FACE FRAMES AND CAP TRIM. For best fit, measure and cut the 1×2 trim as you go. Glue the top and bottom rails to the sides and tack them down with 1¼-inch nails. Then measure, cut, and install the top and bottom rails at the foot of the bed. Next up: all the stiles. Install the middle rails last. For the cap trim, set a miter saw to 45 degrees and cut the footboard ends of the two 1×2s that cap the sides. Cut the other ends at 90 degrees. Glue and nail the side caps in place. Now measure for the footboard cap, set the saw back to 45 degrees, and miter both ends to fit. Glue and nail, as above, with 1¼-inch nails.

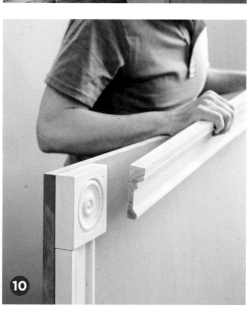

10_ INSTALL THE HEADBOARD TRIM. Glue and tack the rosettes in place at the corners. Measure between each one and the platform and cut the door casing to length. Use a jigsaw or a Japanese handsaw to notch the casings around the side panels, and glue and nail them in place. Then install the horizontal piece of casing between the rosettes. Finally, cut a ½×3 lattice strip to fit between the support frame and the horizontal casing. Center it from side to side, and glue and nail it in place.

11_ INSTALL THE PANELING. Cut the beadboard panels to fit in the two open areas on the headboard between the casing and the lattice strip; affix with construction adhesive and tack down with 1-inch nails. Repeat for all the areas in the face frames with exposed MDF.

12_ ADD THE FINISHING TOUCHES. Use a miter saw to cut quarter-round molding for each side: straight at the headboard end and angled at 45 degrees at the footboard end. Secure the pieces with 1¼-inch nails, then measure, cut, and install the footboard piece. Fill any nail holes, then sand and paint the bed.

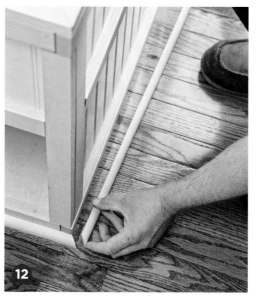

FROM LEFT Custom-built closets, shelves, and dressers can fit in where ceiling height starts to diminish.

This clever combo contains deep drawers under the bed and bookshelves on the desk side of the headboard.

Two shelving units create an alcove that's perfectly sized for an antique dresser.

A bed can be the centerpiece of a wall of cabinetry, adding architectural interest where there was none.

MORE BEDROOM STORAGE

IF THERE IS ONE AREA where most houses fall short, it has to be closet space. And nowhere is that more problematic than in the bedroom. The older the home, the fewer closets you may find. Bedrooms in houses built before 1945 might have only one small shelf-and-rod closet. Maybe the master bedroom contains two slightly larger closets. But that's just a fraction of what the typical family needs nowadays. And because of the way closets fit into the floor plan, there is rarely a practical way to enlarge them. Luckily, bedroom built-ins offer a viable and attractive alternative for accommodating your wardrobe. You can expand your clothes storage by tucking cubbies and drawers into the room's corners, alcoves, and eaves—or even the bed's headboard and mattress base.

Below each swing-arm sconce is an adjustable reading light. →

← WALL-TO-WALL
No room for walk-in closets? These built-in wardrobes yield more storage capacity—and add more character.

← FULLY INTEGRATED
Under-the-bed drawers and bedside cabinets with shelves on top put storage space where there usually is none—all within the footprint that a standard bed and nightstands would have occupied.

→ FLOATING NIGHTSTANDS In a compact room with limited circulation space, two open cubbies provide bedside storage without taking up any square footage.

TRIM TRICK
To support wall-hung shelving units, attach brackets underneath, and fasten them to the wall framing.

Books are accessible but cannot be knocked off the shelf during sleep.

↑STORAGE HEADBOARD Floating a bed in the middle of the room allows for a deep headboard cabinet that combines a nightstand-like tabletop surface, end-cap bookshelves, and spacious dresser drawers.

→WALL OF SHELVING
An upholstered headboard backs up comfortably to bookshelves that offer display space for favorite collectibles and pretty knickknacks.

TRIM TRICK
Using fluted moldings subtly enhances a bookcase face frame without adding any more work for the carpenter.

→SHOE BOXES
In a space too shallow for a full-scale built-in wardrobe, cubbies hidden behind doors offer the perfect spot for organizing footwear.

>CREDITS

FRONT COVER: Eric Roth
BACK COVER: (from left) John Gruen; Alex Hayden (2)
p. 1: (from left) Julian Wass; Susan Teare; Julian Wass
p. 2: (from left) Alex Hayden; Nathan Kirkman; Andrea Rugg
p. 3: (from left) Alex Hayden; Deborah Whitlaw Llewellyn; Spike Powell/GAP Interiors
p. 5: Eric Roth
p. 7: Keller + Keller
p. 8: (from left) Helen Norman; Eric Roth
p. 9: (from left) Anthony Tieuli; Alex Hayden
p. 10: Eric Roth
p. 11: Paul Markert/Collinstock; (illustration) Gregory Nemec
p. 12: Laurey W. Glenn
p. 13: Eric Roth
p. 14: (from left) Eric Roth; Alex Hayden
p. 15: (from left) Wendell T. Webber; Eric Roth
p. 16: (from left) Tria Giovan; John Granen
p. 17: Casey Dunn
p. 18: Wendell T. Webber
p. 19: (illustration) Gregory Nemec
pp. 20-21: Wendell T. Webber
p. 22: (from left) Laurey W. Glenn; Rob D. Brodman
p. 23: (from left) Simon Whitmore/IPC Images; Laura Moss
p. 24: Eric Roth
p. 25: (clockwise from top left) Jake Fitzjones/IPC Images (2); Alan Shortall (2)
p. 26: (from left) Thomas J. Story; Alan Shortall/Cornerhouse Stock
p. 27: Alex Hayden
p. 29: John Granen
p. 30: (from left) David Prince; David Fenton
p. 31: (from left) Dominique Vorillon; Nathan Kirkman
p. 32: Ken Gutmaker
p. 33: Nathan Kirkman
p. 34: (from left) David Fenton; Ken Gutmaker
p. 35: Courtesy of Crown Point Cabinetry
p. 36: Helen Norman
p. 37: (from left) Paul Dyer; Beth Singer
p. 38: (from left) Helen Norman; Paul Whicheloe
p. 39: (from top) Eric Roth; Julian Wass; Alexandra Rowley
p. 40: (from left) Alex Hayden; Susan Teare
p. 41: (from left) David Prince; Nathan Kirkman
p. 42: Sara Essex
p. 43: Paul Dyer
p. 44: Brian Gomsak
p. 45: (from left) Susan Gilmore; Jack Thompson
p. 46: (from left) Jason Varney; Nathan Kirkman
p. 47: David Prince
p. 49: Deborah Whitlaw Llewellyn
p. 50: (from left) Alex Hayden; Laurey W. Glenn
p. 51: (from left) Laurey W. Glenn; Erik Johnson
p. 52: Keller + Keller
p. 53: Alex Hayden
p. 54: Keller + Keller
p. 55: Nathan Kirkman; (illustration) Gregory Nemec
p. 56: (from left) Janis Nicolay; Laurie Black/Collinstock
p. 57: (from top) Greg Premru; Joe Schmelzer; Andrea Rugg/Collinstock
p. 58: (from left) J. Curtis; Andrea Rugg
p. 59: (from left) Alex Hayden; Tria Giovan
p. 60: John Ellis
p. 61: (from left) Robin Stubbert/GAP Interiors; Andrew Bordwin
p. 62: (from left) Mark Lohman; Chad Holder
p. 63: Deborah Whitlaw Llewellyn
p. 64: (from left) Douglas Gibb/GAP Interiors; Laura Moss
p. 65: (from top) Eric Piasecki; Olson Photographic/Cornerhouse Stock; Nick Carter/GAP Interiors
p. 66: (from left) Laura Moss; David Prince
p. 67: (from left) Deborah Whitlaw Llewellyn; Laura Moss
p. 68: (from left) John Ellis; Laura Moss
p. 69: Ryan Kurtz
p. 70: Julian Wass
p. 71: (from left) Steve Randazzo; David Prince
p. 72: Wendell T. Webber; (illustration) Gregory Nemec
p. 73: Reena Bammi
p. 75: John Granen
p. 76: (from left) Michael Luppino; Ken Gutmaker
p. 77: (from left) Tria Giovan; Matthew Millman
p. 78: (from left) Julian Wass; Casey Dunn
p. 79: David Prince
p. 80: Mark Lohman
p. 81: John Gruen; (illustration) Gregory Nemec
p. 82: Tria Giovan
p. 83: Alex Hayden
p. 84: (from left) Ivan Hunter/Getty Images; Nathan Kirkman
p. 85: (from left) Dominique Vorillon; Joe Schmelzer
p. 86: (from left) Graham Atkins-Hughes/IPC Images; Eric Roth
p. 87: Keller + Keller
p. 88: (clockwise from top left) Eric Roth (2); Susan Teare (2)
p. 89: Deborah Whitlaw Llewellyn
p. 90: Ryan Benyi; (illustration) Gregory Nemec
p. 91: Ryan Benyi
p. 92: (from left) Aimee Herring; Jessie Walker/Cornerhouse Stock
p. 93: (from left) Nathan Kirkman; Alexandra Rowley
p. 94: (from left) Bruce Buck; Julian Wass
p. 95: Aimee Herring
p. 96: (from left) Deborah Whitlaw Llewellyn; Mark Samu
p. 97: (from top) Thomas J. Story; Trevor Richards/IPC Images; Eric Piasecki
p. 99: Keller + Keller
p. 100: (from left) Tom McWilliam; Alex Hayden
p. 101: (from left) Alex Hayden; Julian Wass
p. 102: Michael Robinson/Beateworks/Corbis

©2012 by Time Home Entertainment Inc.
135 West 50th Street
New York, NY 10020

ISBN 10: 0-8487-3499-8
ISBN 13: 978-0-8487-3499-2

Library of Congress Control Number: 2012940875

Printed in the United States of America
First Printing 2012

Oxmoor House
Vice President, Publishing Director: **Jim Childs**
Editorial Director: **Leah McLaughlin**
Creative Director: **Felicity Keane**
Brand Manager: **Fonda Hitchcock**
Managing Editor: **Rebecca Benton**

This Old House
Easy Upgrades: Built-ins, Shelves, and Storage
Editor: **Kathryn Keller**
Design Director: **Hylah Hill**
Art Director: **Michele Walthers**
Photo Editor: **Allison Chin**
Writer: **Josh Garskof**
Technical Editor: **Thomas Baker**
Deputy Art Director: **Douglas Adams**
Managing Editor: **Jeff Nesmith**
Editorial Production Manager: **Yoshiko Taniguchi-Canada**
Copy Editor: **Janet Kim**
Proofreader: **Brenda Campbell**
Editorial Intern: **Amanda L. Shettleton**
Art Intern: **Teppei Masuda**
Prepress Coordinator: **Robert Thompson**
Prepress Manager: **Ann-Michelle Gallero**
Book Production Manager: **Susan Chodakiewicz**

To order additional publications,
call 1-800-765-6400 or 1-800-491-0551.

For more books to enrich your life, visit **oxmoorhouse.com**.

To subscribe to *This Old House* magazine, go to
thisoldhouse.com/customerservice or call 1-800-898-7237.

This Old House Magazine
Editor: **Scott Omelianuk**
Publisher: **Charles R. Kammerer**

EDITORIAL
Deputy Editor: **Kathryn Keller**
Managing Editor: **Jeff Nesmith**
Building Technology Editor: **Thomas Baker**
Design Editor: **Colette Scanlon**
Features Editor: **Amy R. Hughes**
Articles Editor: **Deborah Baldwin**
Senior Editor: **Deborah Snoonian**
Senior Technical Editor: **Mark Powers**
Staff Editor: **Amy Roberts**
Associate Editor: **Keith Pandolfi**
Assistant Editor: **Sal Vaglica**
Editorial Assistant: **Megan Baker**
Copy Chief: **Timothy E. Pitt**
Deputy Copy Chief: **Leslie Monthan**
Special Projects Editor: **Eric Hagerman**
Senior Contributor: **Mark Feirer**
Editorial Assistant and Assistant to the Editor: **Gillian Barth**

ART
Design Director: **Hylah Hill**
Director of Photography: **Denise Sfraga**
Deputy Art Director: **Douglas Adams**
Associate Photo Editor: **Allison Chin**
Assistant Art Director: **Cynthia Ng**
Designer: **Paris Osgerchian**
Art/Online Assistant: **Robert Hardin**

EDITORIAL PRODUCTION
Editorial Production Manager: **Yoshiko Taniguchi-Canada**

ONLINE
Online Editor: **Alexandra Bandon**
Web Designer: **Bill Mazza**
Associate Editor: **Tabitha Sukhai**
Contributing Producer: **Elizabeth Lilly**
Contributor: **Karen Ziga**

EDITORIAL BOARD
Master Carpenter: **Norm Abram**
General Contractor: **Tom Silva**
Plumbing and Heating Expert: **Richard Trethewey**
Landscape Contractor: **Roger Cook**
Host: **Kevin O'Connor**